TIGER
LORD OF THE JUNGLE

Tiger, Lord of the Jungle
First published in the United Kingdom by
Evans Mitchell Books
The Old Forge
Forge Mews
16 Church Street
Rickmansworth
Hertfordshire WD3 1DH
United Kingdom

Photography copyright © 2010: Alain Pons
except illustration and photography:
- page 14 (bottom), 26, 27: Éric Pierre
- page 31: François Moutou
- page 54: Christine Baillet
- page 78, 79 (top), 80, 81, 82 (top): Henri Ciechowski
- page 98: Antique print of royal tiger, elephants, betel nut palm tree from *The Instructive Picture Book* (1867)
- page 99: Alain Benainous/Gamma/Eyedea
- page 108 (top): Pallava Bagla/Unep/Still Pictures/Bios
- page 108 (bottom): Belinda Wright

Text copyright © 2010: François Moutou

Graphic design: Empreinte & Territoires, Paris, France
Pre-press: Fotimprim, Paris, France

Translation: Caroline Taggart

All rights reserved. No part of this publication may be reproduced, stored in a retrieval system or transmitted in any form or by any means, electronic, mechanical, photocopying or otherwise, without the prior written consent of the publisher.

British Library Cataloguing in Publication Data
A CIP record of this book is available on request from the British Library.

ISBN: 978-1-901268-40-9

Printed in Thailand

TIGER
LORD OF THE JUNGLE
ALAIN PONS & FRANÇOIS MOUTOU

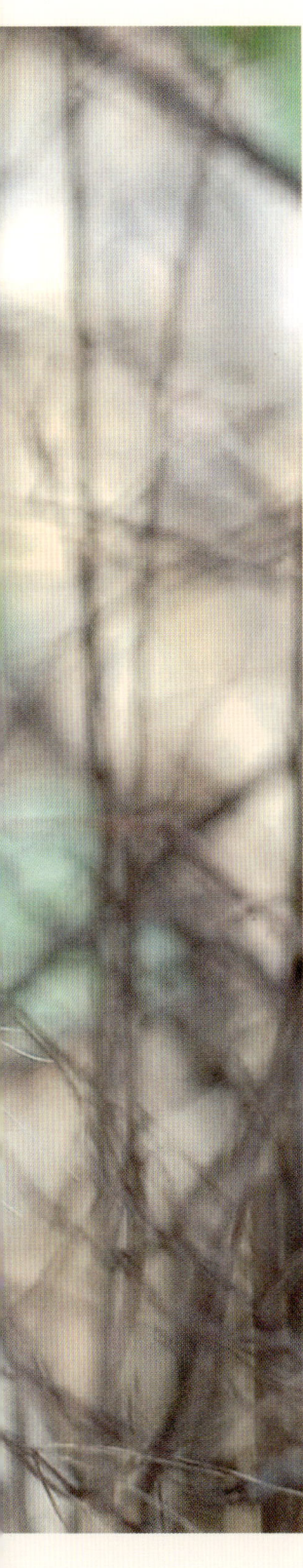

CONTENTS

6   INTRODUCTION

10   ASIA'S BIG STRIPED CAT

24   FROM SNOWY WASTES TO STEAMY JUNGLES

38   TERRITORY AND COMPETITION

58   IN THE TIGER'S SIGHTS

76   PRIVATE LIVES

96   OF TIGERS AND MEN

112   THE UNWRITTEN FUTURE

126   RECOMMENDED READING AND ACKNOWLEDGEMENTS

INTRODUCTION

The tiger is one of the most easily recognised of all wild animals. Few people would hesitate before coming up with the name of the big striped cat. However, recognition is not the same as comprehension. Today the species faces major challenges in terms of our understanding of its needs and our efforts to preserve it. No one knows how it will all end. We still do not know enough about the tiger's biology, ecology and behaviour to be able to claim to understand it, or to have a chance of protecting it and ensuring its survival for future generations. In addition, its distribution, which as recently as the start of the 20th century stretched from eastern Turkey to the Pacific Ocean, and from central Asia to the island of Bali, has shrunk enormously. It is estimated that the tiger now occurs in as little as 7 per cent of its former range. More often than not, it is found in small, residual populations, isolated from each other and in danger of disappearing in the not too distant future. The reasons are always the same: destruction of habitat, scarcity of prey, hunting, disease, poaching for trophies or for use in traditional medicine. How do we account for the fact that such an iconic species has suddenly found itself in such a delicate and tragic position? The purpose of this work is neither to judge nor to condemn, but instead to illustrate as colourfully as possible the richness of the knowledge we do have of a species that is particularly symbolic of the world's wildlife, and its prospects as they appear to us now, at the start of the

21st century. The term 'biodiversity' is on everyone's lips, but what are we actually doing about it? Many of the questions raised by the tiger in Asia apply equally to innumerable other species scattered throughout the world. The reasons for preserving this diversity – whether it be of plants or animals, on land or sea, diurnal or nocturnal, familiar or unfamiliar – are many, varied and widely known. What is lacking is a global will to clarify these reasons and to draw rapid conclusions from them.

This may be the result of (simple) negligence, (false) complacency or (bad) habits. Leafing through these pages, reading the text, looking at the astonishing images that accompany it, is perhaps a first step towards asking ourselves the questions that may lead to an answer. Let us make one thing clear.

The tigers are not asking anyone to come and study them. They are not asking anything at all except to be left alone, to live their lives; but if we were to achieve no more than that it would be no bad thing. From these seven chapters and numerous photographs, most of them taken in the Indian jungle, we hope that something of the tiger's history, recent past and present will emerge, and that this will pave the way to ensuring that it has a future. The first chapter describes the species by recalling where it came from and following its historical distribution pattern. The second introduces the different types

of forest that form its typical habitat. The third chapter describes the social life of this solitary creature and sheds light on this apparent contradiction. The fourth concentrates on the physical characteristics that enable the tiger to capture the prey on which it feeds, from the tiny muntjac deer to the imposing gaur. In chapter five we go behind the scenes of the great cat's family life, with its brief courtships and long periods devoted to raising young. The last two chapters summarise several thousand years of tigers and humans living side by side, including some happy memories, some more sombre ones, and trying to end on an optimistic note. The lot of the other large carnivores is not much more enviable than the tiger's. Not so long ago the lion – now closely associated with the African savannah – was still to be found in the Near and Middle East. One population survives in the Gir forest of north-west India, making this the only country that is home to both of the world's two biggest cats. Over the centuries, many peoples have lived alongside the tiger; some continue to do so. Most have been so influenced by it that their culture makes use of its name, its image, its symbolism. Living in such close proximity is not always entirely serene, but these people take the consequences, and ask also to be left alone. A symbol of strength, courage and ferocity, the tiger could equally well become an image of peace, of successful coexistence – which would present a new challenge for this remarkable creature.

ASIA'S BIG STRIPED CAT

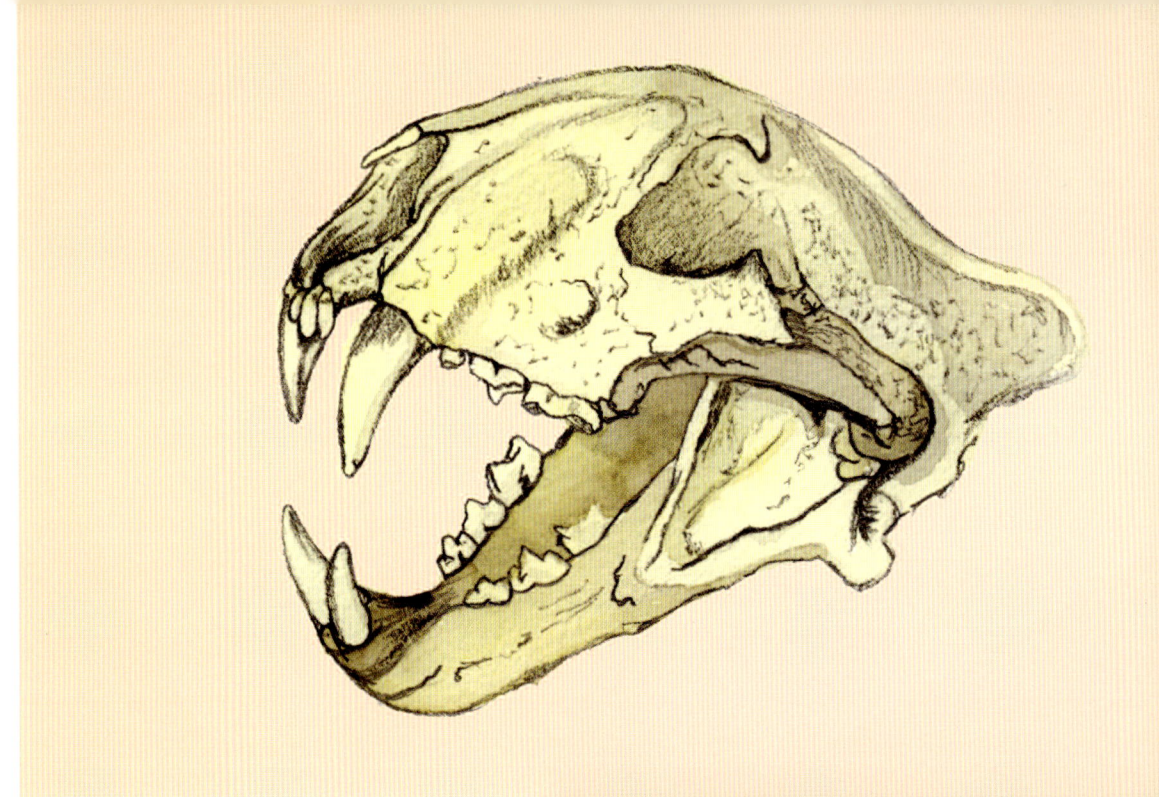

Sabre-toothed tigers must have been impressive. However, we still don't know how they used their gigantic canines. In addition, they weren't real tigers, but belonged to another group of carnivores, some of which resembled modern cats.

Tigers are big cats; that is to say that they are members of the zoological family Felidae, the order Carnivora and the class Mammalia. They are the only big cats with a striped coat and there is only one species, *Panthera tigris*, which emerged from the heart of the Asian continent. The carnivores are characterised by the anatomical traits they have in common, especially those to do with their teeth. The particularly strongly developed fourth upper premolar and first lower molar, called carnassials, are present in all carnivores, living or fossil. The order is of ancient origin. One of the earliest known fossils, *Miacis*, dates from the Eocene epoch, at the very beginning of the Tertiary era; that is, about 55 million years ago (mya). In the course of time, the carnivores gradually diversified to create the present families and those of the recent past. The first known felid, *Proailurus*, dates from about 30 mya.

12

Photographed in Ranthambhore National Park in India – one of the best places for observing tigers – this young male pays close attention to visitors to his territory, looking away only when he is satisfied that they mean no harm.

Between the Sumatran tiger with its prominent side whiskers (above left), the archetypal Indian tiger (above right) and the Siberian tiger with its thick fur (below), there may not be many differences. The species' history is quite recent and not all scientists recognise the various subspecies.

Over tens of millions of years, another family, bearing a close resemblance to the felids, developed alongside them. These were the Nimravidae. Looking rather like lions and tigers, some had two sabre-like upper canines. They became extinct about 2 mya, leaving no descendants. During the Pliocene a carnivorous marsupial, *Thylacosmilus atrox,* appeared in South America and also had overdeveloped canines. The pros and cons of such teeth are still the subject of debate. Among the felids, other 'sabre-toothed tigers' evolved, notably the genera *Homotherium* and *Smilodon,* the former in the Old World, the latter in the New, and they survived up until the beginning of the Quaternary era (about 1.8 mya). These animals raise some questions for evolutionary specialists. It seems likely that natural selection among sabre-toothed tigers aimed to make the act of predation as efficient as possible, even at

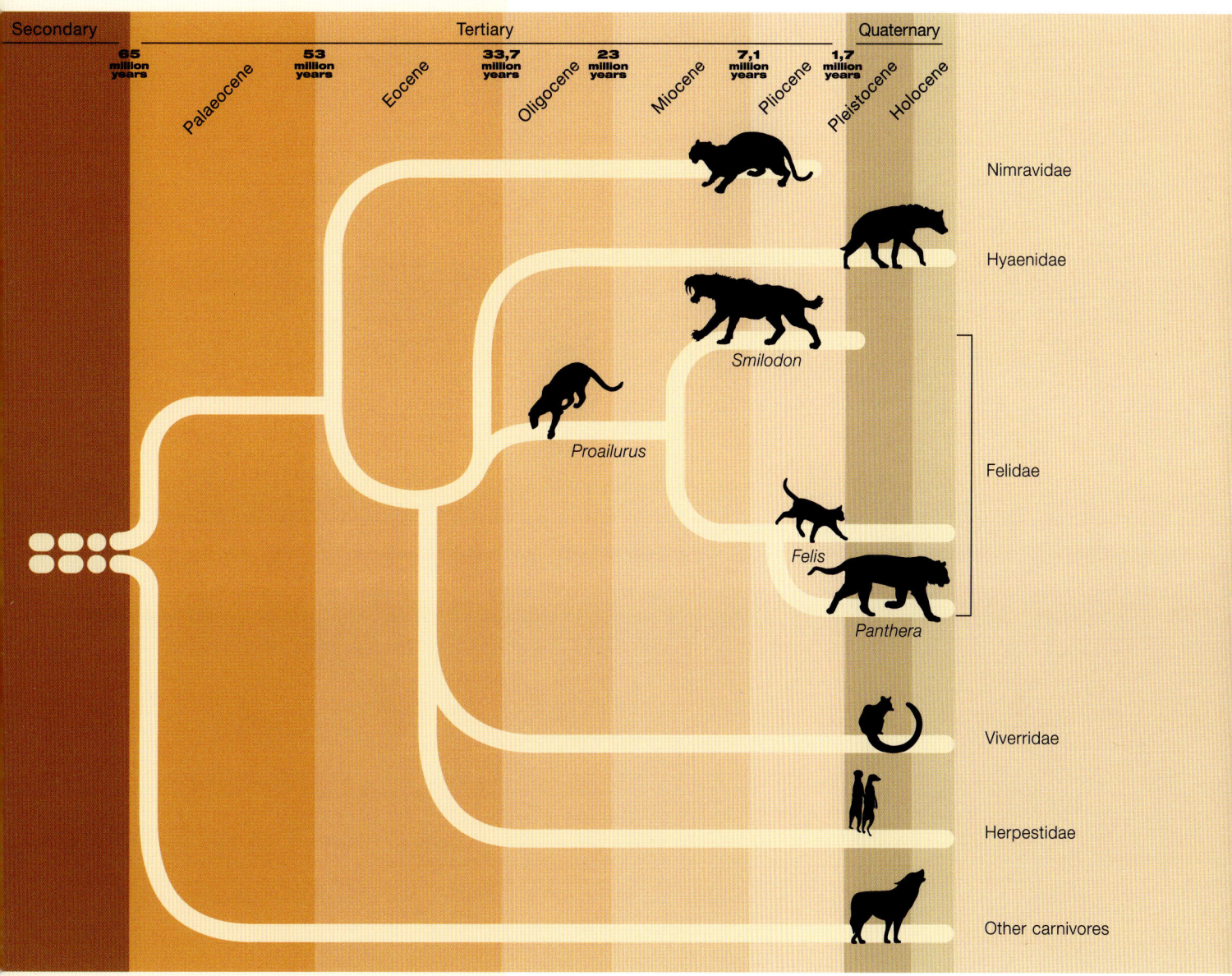

the expense of a powerful bite: having to keep the mouth wide open in order to be able to use those long teeth made them a bit of an inconvenience! In contrast, among other felids, selection tended towards a strong bite and more or less uniform pressure, no matter what the species or what size it was.

As for the tiger, whose origin and distribution have always been confined to Asia, it is the largest cat of the genus *Panthera* and also the largest felid that has ever lived. It must have evolved in central China, about 1.5-2 mya, at the time when it separated from the branch that produced the leopard.

Before that, at the beginning of the Pleistocene (about 1.6 mya), there existed a smaller cat, *P. palaeosinensis*, which was either an ancestor of the tiger or a close relative. Beneath their fur, the species of the genus *Panthera*, such as the lion and the leopard, are very like one another. It is difficult to distinguish the skeleton or the fossil remains of a tiger from those of a lion. All adult *Panthera* have a similar skull, with 30 teeth. Because fossil remains are often incomplete and their state of preservation varies greatly, it is difficult for palaeontologists to piece together the species' history. And skeletons tell us nothing about colours, nor about whether the coat was a single colour, striped or spotted! Today's scientists recognise nine subspecies of tiger, of which three have disappeared and the others are all in a critical situation. The most recent was discovered only in 2004 in the Malay Peninsula, at the south of the isthmus of Ka. This ribbon of land separates the populations of the south from those of the north, limiting the interchanges between them and condemning them to genetic isolation. The subspecies are very similar from the morphological point of view; they are distinguished with the help of bio-geographical and genetic data.

Waking from a nap, a young tiger stretches (above left), peaceably showing its claws. Taking a nap also enables it to rest the cushioned 'toes' on which it walks (below). Yawning reveals the six incisors in each jaw and the canines – whose length commands respect! Also visible are the sharp, horny papillae on the tongue which enable the tiger to lick muscle off the bones of a kill.

Nevertheless, a male Nepalese tiger weighs an average of 100 kg (220 lb) more than his Sumatran counterpart, and a female 50 kg (110 lb) more. Starting from the west and working east, the first subspecies was the Caspian tiger *(P. tigris virgata)*, which was once found from Turkey to Chinese Turkestan. In India lives the Bengal tiger *(P. t. tigris)*, in South-east Asia the Corbett or Indo-Chinese *(P. t. corbetti)*. The new Malaysian subspecies has been called Jackson's tiger *(P. t. jacksoni)*.

The classification of tiger subspecies is subject to debate

The central and southern Chinese subspecies *(P. t. amoyensis)* is on the edge of extinction: it has probably vanished from the wild, but still exists in captivity. The Siberian tiger *(P. t. altaica)* is the most impressive of all. Finally, three of the islands of Indonesia are or used to be home to their own subspecies: *P. t. sumatrae* in Sumatra, *P. t. sondaica* (extinct) in Java and *P. t. balica* (extinct) in Bali. Some specialists believe that the cited differences are hardly enough to divide the species into subspecies. At the other extreme, some have suggested recognising the tigers of the islands of Indonesia and Malaysia as so many individual species, distinct from the continental tiger. The most interesting aspect of all this is perhaps to be found in the analysis of the tiger's history, using the available palaeontological and morphological information enriched with recent genetic data. The striped cat appears to have emerged in China and *P. t. amoyensis* may represent the ancestral form, or the one closest to it. From there, it seems recently to have conquered Asia as a result of two distinct movements.

Even without a run-up, the tiger is capable of quite a spring, thanks to its powerful hindquarters. This sequence also shows how it uses its tail for balance. Nevertheless, tigers are quite happy to get their feet wet when they feel like it.

The first, towards the west and south of the Himalayas, produced the Indo-Chinese, island and Bengal forms, reaching the Indian subcontinent only 6,000-12,000 years ago. The second, towards the east, produced the Siberian tiger, about 10,000 years ago. From this second movement, a branch forking off to the west and following the same natural corridor as the ancient Silk Route ended up as the Caspian tiger. This migratory axis, between the Tibetan Plain and the Gobi Desert in Mongolia, would have allowed tigers to reach favourable areas further west without settling along the length of the corridor. That is why the geographical range of the Caspian tiger is completely isolated from that of the other subspecies. At the genetic level, the Caspian is very close to the Siberian tiger and differs more from the Bengal subspecies, despite being a nearer neighbour.

The tiger's hunting equipment is as impressive as it is effective, since each adult has to be completely self-sufficient. The proportions of the various parts of its body may not be exactly the same as those of a domestic feline, but the tiger is nevertheless a big cat! Fed normally, our pets do not exceed 5 kg (11 lb), while an adult tiger can weigh 300 kg (660 lb). Depending on individuals and populations, a tiger's weight may vary from 80-325 kg (175-720 lb). It may be 1.5-3 m (5-10 ft) long, with the tail and the height at the shoulder reaching about 1 m (3ft 3 in). Although capable of very powerful leaps, the tiger is not a long-distance runner. It has been measured as jumping a distance of 8-10 m (26-33 ft), though 5-6 m (16-20 ft) is more usual. Its muscular structure allows it to run several metres in as many seconds – necessary for capturing prey after it has stalked close enough to it. If its intended victim escapes, it doesn't pursue it.

The way a tiger's shoulders roll when it walks shows off its beautiful musculature

The forepaws, with their five retractable claws (the hind paws have only four) can 'hug' prey, thanks to the positioning of the collarbone at the front of the shoulder which makes these cats skilful at using their 'hands' and 'arms'. In addition, the power of a tiger's limbs makes it very adept at climbing trees. When cyclones passed through the Gulf of Bengal, the tigers

Despite their size and coat, which one might think would make them easy to spot, tigers have no difficulty remaining out of sight in the shadows of their beloved jungle, or in the clearings, thirsty for the monsoon rains, which they sometimes cross. They show themselves or remain hidden according to their mood.

These portraits of Indian tigers in the wild give the impression that they are placid animals – an impression which doesn't necessarily accord with the reality of a tiger's life as we now know it.

of the Sundarbans survived the sudden rising of the water level simply by hauling themselves up on to branches. Very few were swept away or drowned. As for the tiger's striped attire, it enables it to melt into the undergrowth of the Asian forests. Between the patches of light and shade, the coat breaks up the animal's outline behind the vegetation. That is why its prey has to rely on its hearing if it is to have any chance of picking out the predator before it attacks.

FROM SNOWY WAS

TES TO STEAMY JUNGLES

The tiger's range, past and present, stretches from the Caspian Sea to the Pacific Ocean. Tigers were once found in very different landscapes – cold, equatorial, temperate and tropical, from rainforest to taiga, from sea level to altitudes above 4,000 m (13,000 ft) in the Himalayas. So, although they are usually associated with 'jungle', the Hindi word for the natural forests of the Indian peninsula, they can live in a wide variety of habitats. This chapter takes us across Asia from east to west and almost from north to

The hills of Manchuria and the taiga of the Ussuri region of Russia don't look like typical tiger habitat, but the big cat is just as relaxed and at home in these frozen landscapes as it is in the jungles of India or the rainforests of Malaya. It may, however, be much more sparsely distributed here.

south to visit some magnificent areas where tigers still live or lived until recently. Their total disappearance from several of these countries is the ultimate illustration of the degradation of primary forest, sacrificed in the name of local development, whether for the benefit of industry, agriculture or urban expansion.

At the start of the 20th century, images of tigers in the snow became familiar through the accounts of the Russian authors Nikolai Baikov *(The Great Van: the life of a Manchurian tiger)* and Vladimir Arsenyev *(The Taiga of Ussuri*, later filmed as *Dersu Uzala* by the great Japanese director Akira Kurosawa).

More recently the American author and essayist Peter Matthiessen published *Tigers in the Snow*, superbly illustrated with photos by Maurice Hornocker, about the Siberian tiger and those who are trying to preserve it. The taiga of the Russian Far East is a distinctive landscape combining broad-leaved trees and conifers. Summers can be hot here; the forest turns green and comes alive with birdsong and with the colours that have lain dormant during the long, hard, snowy winter which tigers withstand thanks to their thick coats. The nearness of the Pacific Ocean makes the climate a little milder in a small part of the Siberian tiger's range. The big cats are sometimes seen on the beaches of the Sea of Japan, to the north of the Korean peninsula in the Russian region of the Ussuri, a tributary of the Amur: the two rivers separate China from Russia.

The tiger is a forest animal, living in the most impenetrable environments. The patches of jungle found in Ranthambhore and Bandhavgarh National Parks in India in particular show both the dense vegetation of these areas and the ease with which the tiger can melt into the scenery. Maintaining these ecosystems and the biodiversity they harbour is essential to the tiger's survival.

In the taiga, the density of tiger population varies from 0.1-1 per 100 km^2 (0.25-2.5 per sq. mile) according to the season and the abundance of prey – wild boars, red deer or eastern roe deer. At the end of the 20th century it was estimated that there were a little over 300 tigers here. Considering the immense area that the tiger occupied barely a century ago, it is sad to think that it has disappeared permanently from the part of its range that lay between the Caucasus and Central Asia in such a short time.

This region has suffered from some tragic economic developments, illustrated most vividly by the spectacular retreat of the Aral Sea, to which is linked a very genuine economic and human catastrophe. The tiger's original habitat here was unusual, comprising dense undergrowth and tall, impenetrable stands of reeds along the great rivers and the Caspian and Aral seas. Unfortunately, even the Aral Sea has almost disappeared! The destruction of the willow and tamarisk forests – a form of vegetation known locally

The forests of Indonesia have dwindled alarmingly, depriving the tiger of one of its most favoured habitats. However, several captive-breeding programmes have been set up to help protect the Sumatran tiger (this page). In China (opposite), there are no wild tigers left in Houhe Reserve, Hubei Province, though they may still have been here as recently as 1990.

as tugai – bordering the Amu Daria and Syr Daria rivers has been nothing less than fatal for the striped cats. These two tributaries of the Aral Sea were diverted to provide water for intensive cotton farming, which involved heavy treatment with chemical pesticides. As for the sea itself, it lost half its surface area and three quarters of its volume, leading to the disappearance not only of the tiger but also of whole fishing villages, and leaving behind a ruined economy and a disaster area. This tiger population was probably originally the most widespread of all. Working from east to west, it lived in the valley of Taklamakan in Chinese Turkistan, on the western slopes of the Tian Shan range, in the Alborz mountains of Iran, in eastern Turkey and in the gallery forests fringing the Euphrates and Tigris rivers. A survey conducted in Iran between 1973 and 1976 found not the slightest trace of a tiger. The reedbeds on the edges of the Caspian Sea have been transformed into agricultural land.

The last known tiger in Iran was killed in 1953 in what has since become the Golestan National Park

Tigers can take advantage of a range of environments within their habitat, resting in either sun or shade, depending on the season and local climate. An animal that seems relaxed out in the open is probably quite confident, neither hungry nor on the lookout for a mate.

Certain biologists were also surprised to discover that the tiger had survived in Turkey until the middle of the 20th century. A survey published in 2004 by the Council of Europe records all the latest data about tigers here: the last authenticated individual was probably killed as late as 1970. Details were published in 1974, along with a photograph of the skin, which has since been lost. More recent sightings have been reported but not confirmed, partly because they took place in Turkish Kurdistan, an inaccessible area where movement is controlled by the army. In South-east Asia, from Myanmar to China and including Malaysia and the islands of Sumatra, Java and Bali, in all three of which tigers once lived, the land used to be covered in lush tropical forest, but clearing for cultivation has brought drastic changes to the landscape. Forests recede and are replaced by enormous rubber or palm-oil plantations.

In Java, the last of a series of photos of a tiger in the wild dates from October 1938, though the subspecies probably survived into the 1950s. In central China, in the province of Hubei, near the birthplace of the entire species, the Houhe Reserve can no longer accommodate a tiger, despite the 10,340 hectares (40 sq. miles) that it covers, the protected areas around it and the adjacent reserve in the province of Hunan. Poaching may have contributed to the tiger's

disappearance since the 1970s. Still very beautiful with its wooded valleys, the area was recently explored as part of a survey that failed to discover any trace of the big cat. In the Taman Negara National Park, in the heart of the Malaysian peninsula, the air in the damp, impenetrable forests is suffocating and sticky. But even in this sweltering heat, the tiger's coat is useful, protecting it on the one hand against the rain and the frequent tropical storms and on the other against blood-sucking creatures. The tiger has nothing to fear from these parasites except a tiny and painless loss of blood.

Walking in the park in the hope of encountering a tiger, you are much more likely to come across one of these creepy-crawlies than a big cat. So while waiting for a tiger you can always study leeches! They too are striped, with light brown lines running longitudinally along their dark red-brown skin. Called tiger leeches, they almost certainly belong to the genus *Haemadipsa*. The tropical forests of Malaysia are among the oldest on the planet. Unaffected by the climatic variations associated with the Quaternary glaciations, they date from the end of the Tertiary era. That is why they

Tigers are clever at using their 'hands'. They combine deftness of paw with a lateral movement made possible by the design of the shoulder. Of all the mammals, only the primates outdo them in this respect.

support such an incredibly rich variety of plant and animal species, which are still far from being completely documented or studied. This does not, however, prevent their constant decline. But tigers are more usually associated with the Indian jungle, where memories of Rudyard Kipling and *The Jungle Book* are still vivid. These forests are subject to the rhythm of the monsoons. The cold, dry winter monsoon blows across the yellowed landscape of the north and north-east, while the wet and warm summer monsoon sweeps the green contours of the south and south-west. Yet the peninsula shows some notable variations, from the Sundarbans on the northern coast of the Bay of Bengal – that is, the mangrove swamp forests of the Ganges and Brahmaputra delta between India and Bangladesh – to the high-altitude forests of Bhutan, where tigers climb to 4,500 m (almost 15,000 ft) in the vegetation of the Himalayas.

Knowing all the regions where tigers live is vital if we are to save them

The tiger's current distribution is no more than a few per cent of what it was only a few decades ago. The remains of the Padam Talav Masjid mosque in Ranthambhore and the twisting paths of Kahna National Park, both in India, will make no difference to this. In addition to actual killings, deforestation constitutes a major threat.

In Nepal, their special refuge is Chitwan National Park, on the Terai plain. In India there is a network of protected areas – reserves and national parks – devoted to the tiger but sometimes with the odds stacked against them. In the north, it is worth mentioning Corbett National Park, in the centre Ranthambhore, Bandhavgarh and Kahna, where the forests are comparatively dry. In the south of the subcontinent, the national parks of Nagarhole, Bandipur and Mudumalai protect a fine stretch of forest which becomes denser during the summer monsoon. It is vital that we know all the regions where tigers survive if we are to locate them, count them and assess their needs. Thanks to a recent census, we can define the Tiger Conservation Landscapes in all the countries where tigers are still found. Analysing these environments – in terms of landscape, animals, vegetation, climate, geology and human impact – helps us to maintain forests and other habitats capable of giving the tiger a home.

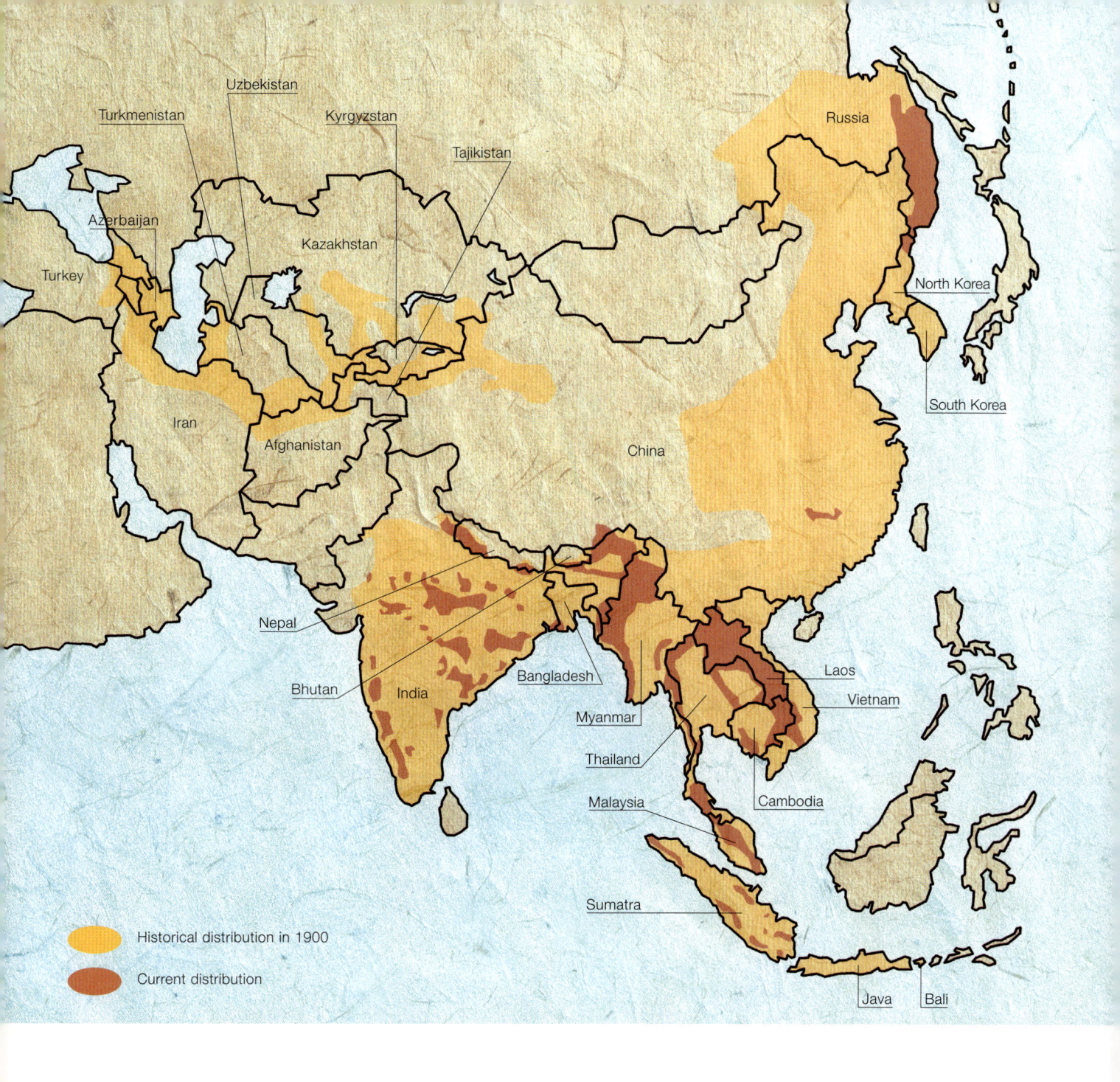

The aim is to repopulate areas that have recently lost their tigers, but that could accommodate them again if the causes of the disappearance were identified and overcome, and above all if the natural habitat made it possible. It's an aim with a lot of ifs, but not necessarily a pipe dream!

TERR

ITORY AND COMPETITION

Territorial and solitary, tigers need vast areas in which to live. But being solitary doesn't mean that individuals don't interact, simply that each one prefers to keep itself to itself. Animals in neighbouring territories know each other, which helps to avoid conflict.

Any territorial animal defends all or part of the area in which it lives, eats, rests and raises its young, keeping other adults of its species away. With tigers, this area covers more or less the whole territory; that is to say, they defend their entire living space. A male's territory, which is more extensive than a female's, can intersect with the territories of as many as three tigresses. The animals live side by side without meeting very often.

Water is an essential ingredient of a tiger's range. In addition, the animal must know every inch of the area it inhabits if it is to have any hope of surviving and raising young. It certainly also knows its nearest neighbours, both male and female, even if each prefers to live alone.

Living a solitary existence does not stop tigers from communicating, often at a distance, with others of their species. Here, a tiger marks its territory with secretions from glands on either side of its mouth, and by spraying jets of urine. These 'scent signals' are deposited at muzzle height, so there is no chance that other tigers passing by will miss them.

To put it simply, two networks of adjacent territories co-exist in a given 'tiger area', one containing larger pieces for the males, the other smaller ones for the females. Territories belonging to two animals of the same sex hardly ever overlap, unless a newly independent female establishes herself not far from her mother and shares a bit of jungle with her. To identify and stake a claim to its space, a tiger marks it with faeces, urinates

Owing a territory is fundamental; without it, a tiger cannot reproduce

on trees or occasionally roars to remind the neighbours that it is still there! It may also scratch the bark of a tree about 3 m (10 ft) above the ground, leaving a visual signal (claw marks) or a scent (secretions from glands in the paws). These marks are usually made on the outskirts of the territory, increasing the chances of their being 'read' by another individual. Sometimes, a powerful roar rings out, bringing a tiger's presence to the attention of any others in the vicinity. Tigers patrol the boundaries of their domain regularly, checking that no one else has come too close and conscientiously maintaining their markers. Inspections are usually carried out at dusk, during the night – in the course of which a tiger may cover 4-10 km (1½-6 miles) – and at dawn. Checking boundaries regularly seems also to be a way of finding out what is happening on the other side. As soon as an individual realises that a neighbour is not around any more, it will try to encroach a little on the other's territory in order to enlarge its own. So a territory never stays vacant for long. In a healthy tiger population, some individuals will be looking for a territory in which to establish themselves, while others, 'property owners', may be feeling that theirs is a little cramped. So the disappearance of one of them very quickly makes some of its near neighbours happy. The average size of a territory is linked to the area an individual needs in order to find enough food all year round, that is about 50 animals the size of an adult deer.

Prey density therefore determines the size of a tiger's territory. That ranges from one tiger per 20 km^2 (8 sq. miles) in Chitwan National Park in Nepal to only one per 450 km^2 (175 sq. miles) in the taiga of the Russian Far East. As a result, tiger density can vary from 16 individuals per 100 km^2 (40 sq. miles)

Tigers patrol their territory regularly to reinforce the signs of ownership and mark strategically positioned trees. They also often choose the same resting places, sheltered but situated so as to allow them to keep an eye on the surrounding area.

in Kaziranga National Park in India to something between 0.1 and 0.4 individuals in the same area of the Sikhote Alin mountains of Siberia. A resident tiger covers the length and breadth of its territory to reassert its right of ownership and to get to know it intimately, to learn where to go at different times of year, to find prey, water, hiding places, cool spots in summer, shelter in winter – all of which increase its chances of surviving, living a long life and being able to reproduce. These factors are particularly important for a female, who has to raise a litter of boisterous and hungry cubs all on her own.

The large living spaces that tigers need and the low reproductive rate of a protected population go some way towards explaining the species' current status. The combination of very low population densities with small increases in numbers means that vast expanses of land must be protected in order to house a population large enough to have a hope of being self-sustaining – a situation that is becoming more and more rare. Even solitary animals need to be able to communicate, if only to avoid each other. Like other cats, tigers make various characteristic sounds such as growling, roaring and purring. Roaring is meant to be heard and understood from a distance, reminding the neighbours that it is best if everyone stays at home. Purring is an intimate sound, used between mother and cubs when they are close together. As cubs are vulnerable for the first few weeks, it is best that no one else is aware of their presence when the tigress goes off to hunt. Unlike domestic cats, tigers have round pupils and usually yellow irises. Their vision is excellent, especially in the half-light.

While resting, a tiger that feels secure and confident will give itself up to some funny positions, not unlike those of a domestic cat. These moments of relaxation are vital, as tigers also occasionally have to make extremely violent efforts. Rest is an important part of the rhythm of a tiger's life. And when it is very hot, shortly before the monsoon, it enjoys the opportunity of lounging close to water.

A tiger's vocalisations often express anxiety or show that it has been disturbed – perhaps by visitors. Tourists and photographers must therefore respect the unwritten rules that prevent the animals from becoming agitated. Even a yawn may indicate a need to release tension.

It is generally the first sense they use when spotting and then approaching prey. But tigers also use their ears if another tiger roars nearby, or if a potential victim gives itself away with a cry. They must also be able to be completely silent, especially when stalking deer, which have particularly sharp hearing.

Like all cats, tigers have handsome whiskers called vibrissae

Several tufts sprout from the muzzle as well as from the cheeks and above the eyes, though the felids are the only carnivores not to have vibrissae on the chin. These long sensitive hairs, with a wealth of nerve endings at the base, are a great asset when the animals are walking in the half-light or dark, in a maze of overgrown jungle. Facing forwards and outwards, vibrissae sense obstacles before they hit the muzzle, the eyes or the top of the head, stopping the tiger from bumping into something or hurting itself. Until the middle of the 20th century, several big cats made their home in India: tigers, lions *(Panthera leo)*, leopards *(P. pardus)*, snow leopards *(P. uncia)*, clouded leopards *(Neofelis nebulosa)* and cheetahs *(Acinonyx jubatus)*. Today the cheetahs have completely disappeared. In all of Asia, there are perhaps thirty or forty left *(A. j. venaticus)* in the central Iranian desert and their future is far from certain.

A young male and his sister sniff interestedly at a scent post. Before long they will separate and the young male will move out of the territory in which he was born.

Tigers often prey on axis deer (Indian chitals); in the forests of the Indian peninsula, peacocks are a less frequent item on the menu.

As for the lion *(P. l. persicus)*, it just hangs on in the Gir forest in north-western India. So the tiger once had serious competitors. Among the carnivores, it also rubs shoulders with four species of bear – the brown bear *(Ursus arctos)*, the Asiatic black bear *(U. thibetanus)* and the sloth bear *(Melursus ursinus)* on the Indian peninsula and the sun bear *(Helarctos malayanus)* in South-east Asia – and has no qualms about attacking any of them should their paths cross.
In Russia, adult brown and black bears appear regularly on the tiger's menu, brought down by spectacular charges. One of the big cat's most amazing neighbours is the dhole *(Cuon alpinus)*, a social canid found in much of tropical and temperate Asia and sometimes called the whistling dog because of its call. As yet we know little about it. Hunting in packs, dholes are capable of driving a tiger away from a kill.

In India, the tiger may come across some impressive neighbours. Although often anxious by nature, the elephants *(Elephas maximus)* of Corbett National Park don't generally have anything to fear from the big cat. In Kaziranga, the great one-horned Indian rhinoceros *(Rhinoceros unicornis)* is always at risk from poachers, despite its protected status.

Because of its choice of prey, the wolf *(Canis lupus)* is a direct competitor of the tiger, unlike the sloth bear *(Melursus ursinus)*, which eats ants, termites and other insects.

Packs have been observed hurting and even killing a tiger, although this does not happen often and the reverse may also occur. As a rule, the large predators prefer to avoid each other. In Asia, tigers may still come across wolves *(Canis lupus)*, rather puny members of the dog family which in the Indian forests generally live in small packs. Of the three Asian leopards, only the 'true' leopard occasionally poses a threat to a tiger – it is usually the other way round. The snow leopard inhabits high mountains where the striped cat is not found. Even in Bhutan, where a tiger has been photographed at an altitude of 4,500 m (almost 15,000 ft), the two species do not meet. The tiger stays under the cover of trees and bushes, while the snow leopard lives and hunts at the next level up, which even in the Himalayas is called alpine.

A brother and sister may spend a few weeks together after leaving their mother but before becoming completely independent. The young male's life is likely to be more adventurous and dangerous than that of the young female, who will probably settle down not far from her mother.

The tiger's coat is good camouflage in the dappled light of the vegetation, while the snow leopard's thick speckled fur hides it against a scree. The clouded leopard, at 10-25 kg (22-55 lb) the smallest of the three and the one found in the most tropical regions, is a tree-dweller and must be unobtrusive wherever it comes into contact with the tiger. It is found in South-east Asia and on Sumatra and Borneo, where it lives alongside the orangutan. The tiger occurs only in Sumatra, and the great ape spends much more time in trees here, where the predator prowls, than in Borneo. The two island populations of orangutan are at the moment regarded as separate species, *Pongo pygmaeus* in Borneo and *P. abelii* in Sumatra. Some specialists also classify the clouded leopard of Borneo and Sumatra as a different species from its continental cousin, respectively *N. diardi* and *N. nebulosa*. Cats are generally thought not to like the water. However, tigers bathe of their own free will. They are also good swimmers and can cross rivers or sea inlets several kilometres wide. When they first spread across Asia, great open spaces such as the prairies or the steppes must have caused them more difficulty than water. In India, when temperatures reach scorching point, tigers bathe to cool off. In South-east Asia the rains are more frequent and tigers have their share of cooling showers.

Tigers can often be seen panting, half immersed in a pool of water

High up in a tree the crested serpent-eagle (Spilornis cheela) waits to pounce on snakes, lizards and frogs. This bird of prey is found throughout India, where it lives alongside the tiger without either interfering with the other.

In Siberia, they have no hesitation about rolling in the winter snow. Their beautiful fur acts as a raincoat and prevents them from catching cold. However, it is siesta time that provides one of the most classic images of the tiger. A tiger must store up a lot of energy to capture its prey, defend its territory and raise its young. To keep fit and remain in control of its territory, it must save its strength. A tiger that looks as if it is taking it easy is in fact recovering from its last hunt or patrol and preparing itself for the next. This tranquillity is of the utmost importance to a female with cubs. Although the male doesn't participate directly in their upbringing, his presence in the vicinity deters other marauding males who may not know the female and may try to kill her offspring. The mere presence of the territorial male protects the living area of the female and her young, who are also his own.

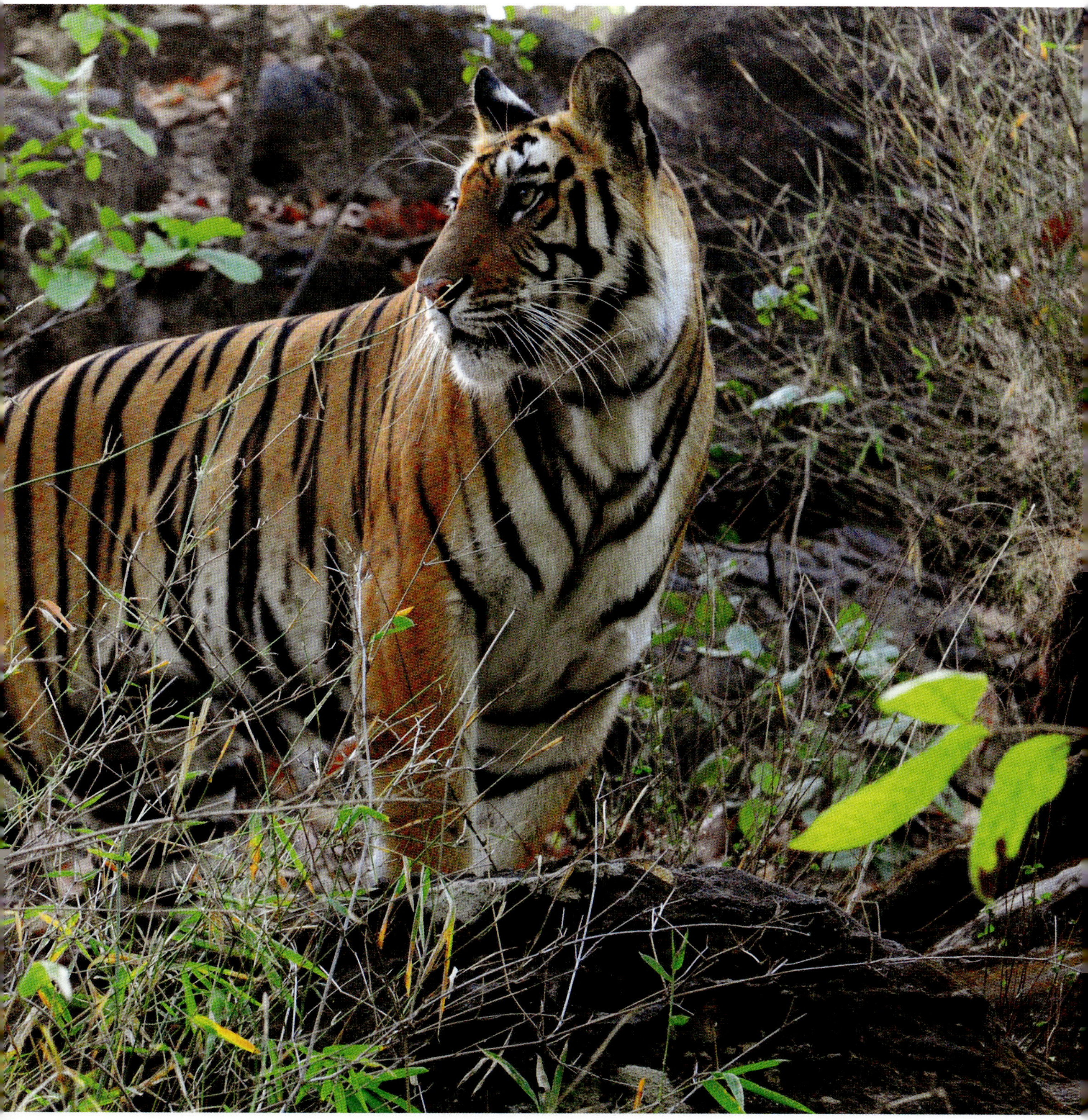

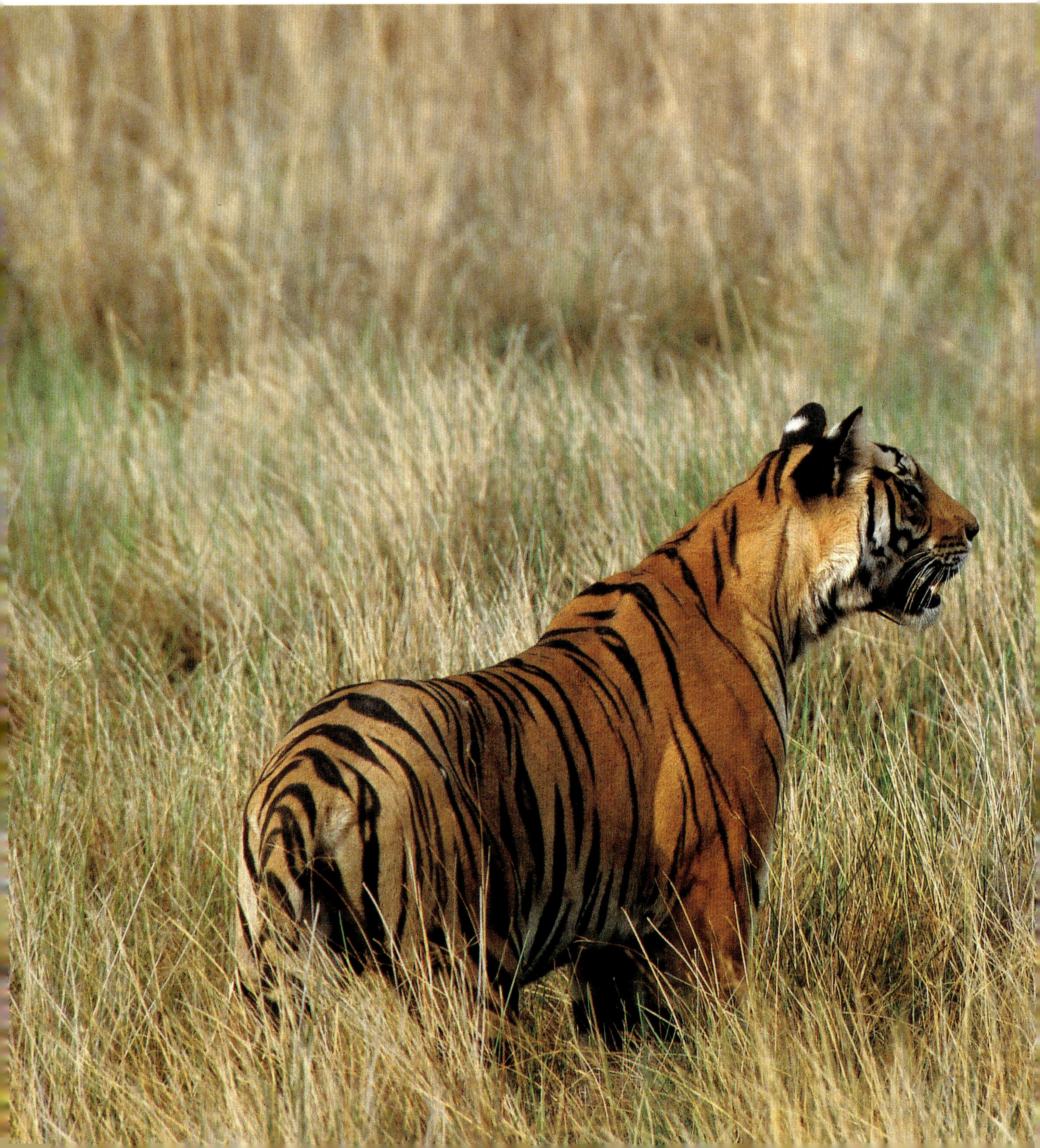

IN THE TIGER'S SIGHTS

As a solo hunter a tiger doesn't have to share its prey, but it does first have to catch it, and that of course is also a solo effort.

Hunting strategy varies according to the environment

Even the mighty gaur – also under threat because of habitat loss – can fall prey to a tiger. The nilgai – a large antelope whose males are grey and females reddish-brown – usually escapes because it prefers open spaces to dense jungle. Having lost two canines, the elderly tigress must adapt her hunting techniques, so important are these four teeth in the capturing and killing of prey.

Wherever it lives, the process is pretty much the same. Sight is the first sense involved in identifying potential prey. But tigers are opportunists and also react to sounds that attract their attention and indicate a possible meal. Next comes the surreptitious approach, during which they use all their guile to keep themselves hidden as long as possible.
A good knowledge of the terrain is indispensable, both to tell them where to look for food and to exploit every aspect of the landscape and vegetation for camouflage.
In the forest there is rarely a strong wind and tigers probably don't need to worry about

60

its direction to avoid being detected by their victims. The final attack, at lightning speed, begins only a few metres away from the target and lasts no more than a few seconds. If the prey escapes this first onslaught, the predator almost never bothers to give chase. Deer can outrun a tiger, but may still be intercepted just as it starts to accelerate. With victims less than half its size, a tiger grasps the back of the neck and breaks it. Other prey is suffocated by pressure to the throat. This cat-like attack and powerful throat bite protect a tiger from the prey's defences, be they teeth, antlers or horns.

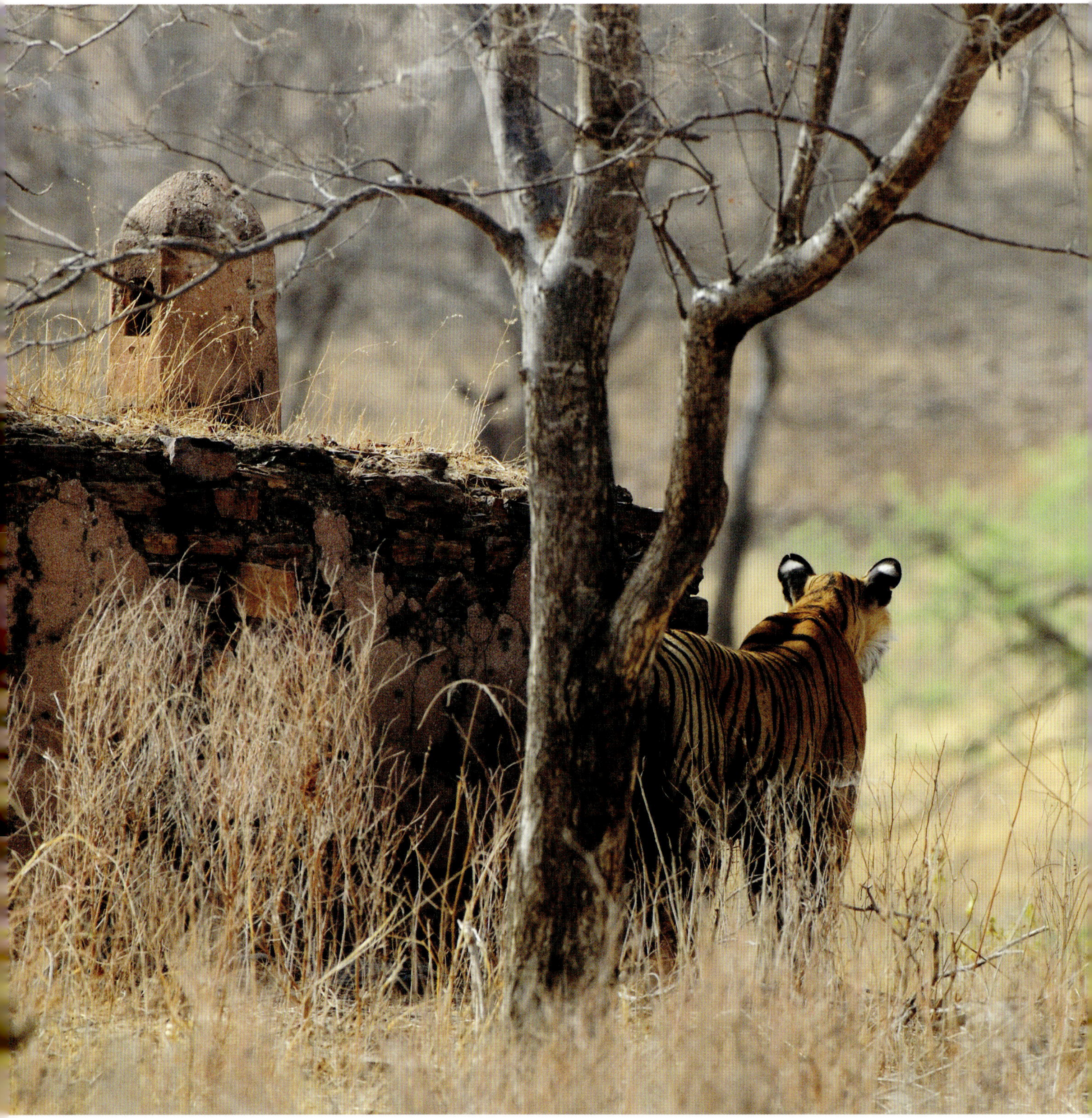

Once captured, the prey is dragged under cover, beneath a bush, away from the covetous eyes of other predators. It is difficult to establish exact figures in the jungle, but it is believed that a tiger may make several dozen attempts before succeeding in making a kill. A young and inexperienced

Prey may hear a tiger in time to run away, or react quickly enough to the final charge

tiger may also make a bad choice and pick on an animal that is too big for it to bring down. With a gaur *(Bos frontalis)*, a species of enormous wild Asian cattle, for example, it may be the tiger that is hurt or even killed. On the other hand, experienced adults can capture practically anything, including young elephants *(Elephas maximus)* or small Indian rhinos *(Rhinoceros unicornis)*. Nevertheless, deer are their most common prey.

Tigers make use of all the features of the landscape, even the remains of manmade ones, in order to move around as unobtrusively as possible and surprise their prey, often chitals. These little deer usually live in small herds, which increases the number of eyes and ears on the alert for danger.

This was shown in one of the first modern studies of the Indian tiger, undertaken by George Schaller in the 1960s and published under the title *The Deer and the Tiger.* The deer may be of different species in different parts of Asia, but the relationship between predator and prey is much the same.

Among this great diversity of deer, which is not found anywhere else, the Siberian roe deer and the red deer *(Cervus elaphus)* live in temperate zones. In Russia the latter is called the maral, but it is an Asian form of the European red deer. Sika deer *(C. nippon),* which prefer subtropical zones, are mainly found in China and Korea. In tropical areas from India to China and Indonesia these are replaced by the sambar *(C. unicolor)* and the Timor deer *(C. timorensis)*. The sambar is a large deer with a single-coloured coat and fairly simple antlers. The slightly smaller Timor deer resembles it and is found on several Indonesian islands. The hog deer *(Axis porcinus)* ranges from Pakistan to South-east Asia but is not found in the southern part of the Indian subcontinent. The little Indian muntjac or barking deer

The common langur is one of the most terrestrial of Asian langurs, which explains why it is a regular part of the tiger's diet. The sambar is a much larger deer than the chital and as such a very tempting prey item: killing a sambar assures the tiger of a slap-up meal.

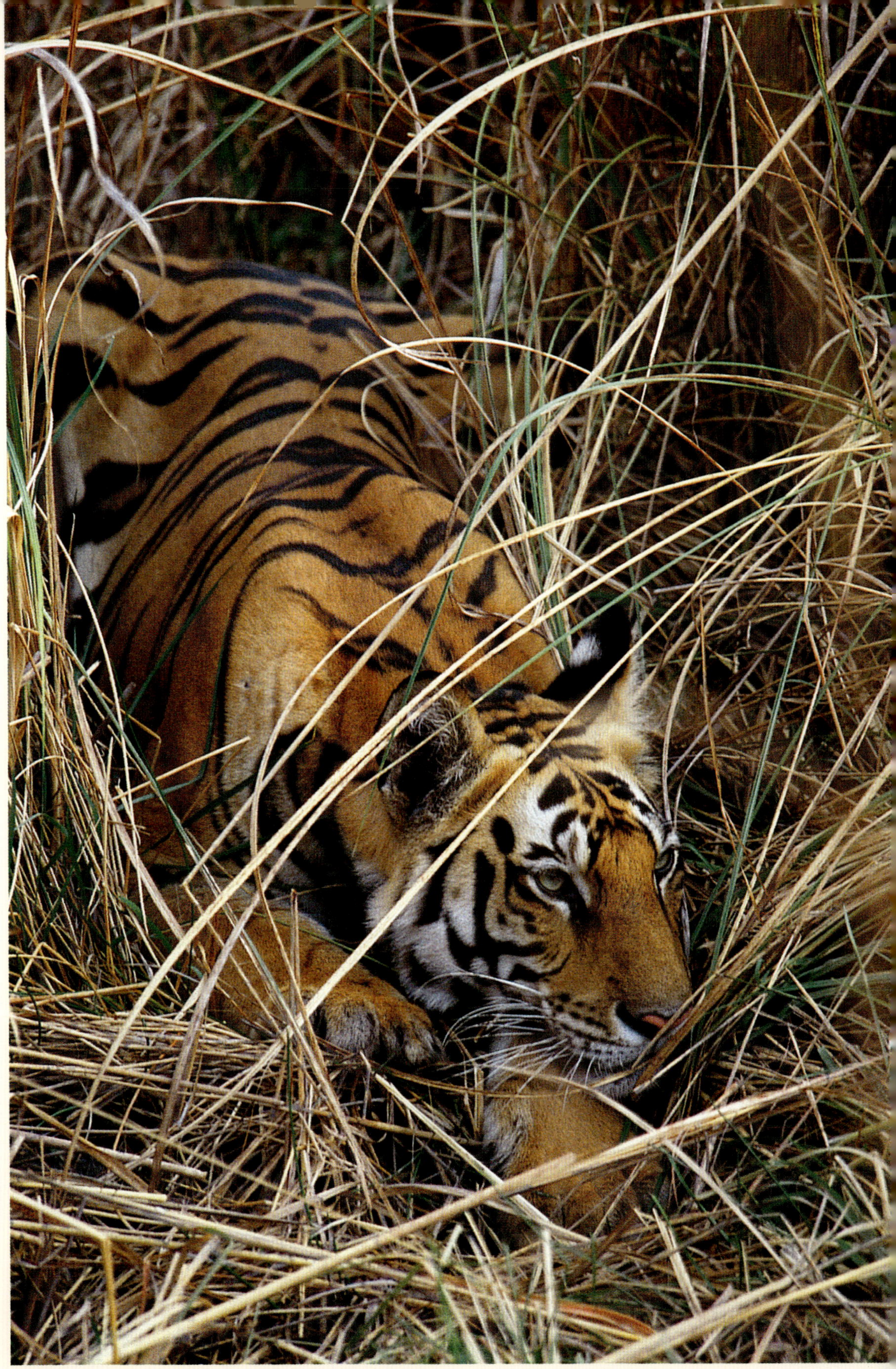

(mainly *Muntiacus muntjak*) is found throughout the hot forest zones of Asia. Adapted to dense undergrowth and bush, and much more solitary than the other Asian deer, it runs with its head down and has minimal antlers. In addition the tiger may prey on more localised species such as the chital or axis deer *(Axis axis)* and the barasinga or swamp deer *(C. duvauceli)*; its survival may even depend on them. This is certainly true of the chital, a beautiful animal with a spotted coat which brightens the undergrowth of the Indian peninsula during the summer monsoon and whose males sport elegant branched antlers. Widespread in southern India, it is a common item on the tigers' menu, especially in Bandipur and Mudumalai national parks. It isn't easy to surprise a deer of any sort, as most live in small herds and this gregarious behaviour helps to protect individuals. Tigers hunt them in tall grass, in the heart of damp tropical forests, in the taiga and even in swamp areas, readily pursuing them into the water.

Although it looks like ideal tiger prey, the little chinkara gazelle generally frequents open country to avoid running into the big cat. When hunting, tigers may stalk with their body close to the ground before pouncing on their victim. They focus intently on their target, ignoring anything else that is going on around them.

This male has just captured a chital (axis deer). As usual, he will feast not on the site of the kill, but a short distance away, under cover and out of sight of envious eyes. Whatever the prey, tigers are capable of summoning up great strength to move their kill to where they want it to be.

The only requirement of the habitat when a tiger is hunting is that it should provide sufficient cover and hiding places for the big cat. Unlike lions, snow leopards and cheetahs, which admittedly live in very different environments, tigers do not hunt in areas of low vegetation. As a result, they rarely take the little Indian gazelles *(Gazella bennettii)*, otherwise known as chinkara, although these do sometimes venture into more covered areas. Another typically Indian species that is rarely hunted is the nilgai *(Boselaphus tragocamelus)*, which makes itself scarce in wooded country. Second in importance to the deer as a prey species, the wild boar (*Sus scrofa*) is found in both tropical zones and coniferous forest. Tigers also occasionally take musk deer (various species of the genus *Moschus*), found from the Himalayan woods to the taiga, and in India regularly eat monkeys, notably the Hanuman

A tiger's teeth perform different functions depending on their shape and their position in the mouth. The carnassials, on the side of the jaw, act like scissors and slice through pieces of meat – hence the side-on bite (opposite). The incisors enable a predator to open up the skin of its victim or to scrape meat from the bones with the help of the tongue (this page).

Although a lone calf makes an easy prey, a tiger does occasionally succeed in bringing down a gaur that weighs close to a tonne (2,000 lb). As for the tapirs, they occupy a limited range around the Malay Peninsula and the island of Sumatra, where tigers are no longer plentiful. There is one last type of prey to which tigers are sometimes forced to resort – domestic cattle. In areas where hunting, poaching and encroachment on space haven't left room for the wild ungulates, nothing but livestock remains. This inevitably sparks a violent reaction from the herdsmen, but the increase in the number of cattle leads to the often irreversible loss of forests and

A tiger may also attack dogs, particularly on the outskirts of villages

large animals, without solving the problems of stock breeders and farmers. A tiger's meal interests a lot of other residents of the jungle or the taiga. But tigers are not great sharers. A sambar can supply food for several days, during which time the predator will stay in the vicinity, both to protect its kill from possible looting and to avoid moving too far between meals. It will sometimes cover its booty with vegetation to protect it from the sun and from the sight of prowlers. The interest expressed by members of the crow family doesn't seem to bother the predator. These 'commensal' animals are able to share its meal without really robbing it. Obviously, if a group of vultures turned up, that would be different.

langur *(Semnopithecus entellus)* – also known as the grey langur – which is found almost all over the country. Large and light-coloured, these langurs sometimes come down from the trees to feed on the ground. Being too noisy can prove fatal. But tigers can also be satisfied with smaller species such as porcupines, hares, peacocks, pheasants and even frogs. In the mangroves of the Sundarbans, they sometimes catch fish, either directly or by filching them from the nets of the local fishermen, who really do not appreciate this. Large species such as the gaur, banteng *(Bos javanicus)*, wild water buffalo *(Bubalus arnee)* or Malayan tapir *(Tapirus indicus)* represent a fearsome challenge for a tiger. The first three are large wild forest cattle whose adults are hard to confront, especially as they live in groups and show a certain solidarity.

Unfortunately, the number of vultures of the *Gyps* genus in India has diminished considerably since the 1990s. They used to feed on the remains of domestic cattle that had frequently been treated with an anti-inflammatory, one of whose ingredients poisoned the birds. More than 90 per cent of the members of three species have disappeared. In India, you may still come across the striped hyena *(Hyaena hyaena)*, the golden jackal *(Canis aureus)* and the Bengal or Indian fox *(Vulpes bengalensis)*, always lying in wait for easy pickings. Like the vultures, these are scroungers. Even so, they have to risk pilfering a kill from under the nose of its owner, without being seen and certainly without being caught. If that happened, the punishment would be conclusive. An adult tiger needs 5-6 kg (11-13 lb) of meat a day, or about 2 tonnes (4,000 lb) a year. But only half its prey is really edible. So it needs a muntjac of 20 kg (44 lb) every two or three days, or a sambar of 200 kg (440 lb) once a fortnight. Because a tiger doesn't catch prey to a fixed timetable, it also eats intermittently, alternating periods of enforced fasting with times of plenty. A hungry tiger may often consume more than 20 kg (44 lb) of meat at its first meal from a fresh kill! But it also needs to drink and it will go off at regular intervals to quench its thirst and digest. In India, a chital of around 100 kg (220 lb) is the ideal prey: it feeds a tiger for about a week. It also guarantees good-quality meat – the larger carcass of a sambar must cease to be very appetising after a few days. So tigers still have the same essential requirements: they need large areas with a variety of habitats – wooded, undisturbed and containing plenty of ungulates.

After a good meal, a tiger needs to drink and groom itself. The horny papillae that cover the top of the tongue make a very efficient brush for cleaning the coat.

Reserves created for them in fact additionally protect a whole battalion of other, often smaller species, adapted to the same environment. So again the most important thing is to protect the natural habitats. Like all predators, tigers can have an impact on the prey species, but the cats seem to be much more dependent on the availability of prey than a threat to the species as

Loss of habitat and of prey is as fatal to the tiger as direct destruction

After eating its fill, a tiger indulges in an energetic grooming session before settling down for a long after-dinner nap. It nevertheless stays close to its kill in case hunger strikes again. A predator's life is a lottery that subjects it to a succession of feasts and famines.

a whole. The cover which tigers need so desperately also protects the soil, ensures a certain distribution of rainfall across the region concerned, reduces the incidence of drought by retaining water long after the rains, slowing down evaporation and feeding the sources of numerous streams and springs. During the torrential summer monsoon, the same forest absorbs part of the overflow, preventing the erosion of fertile soil. In return, correctly exploited, the forest provides wood, fruits, plants and its cavalcade of animals. Protecting the tiger means much more than protecting a single species.

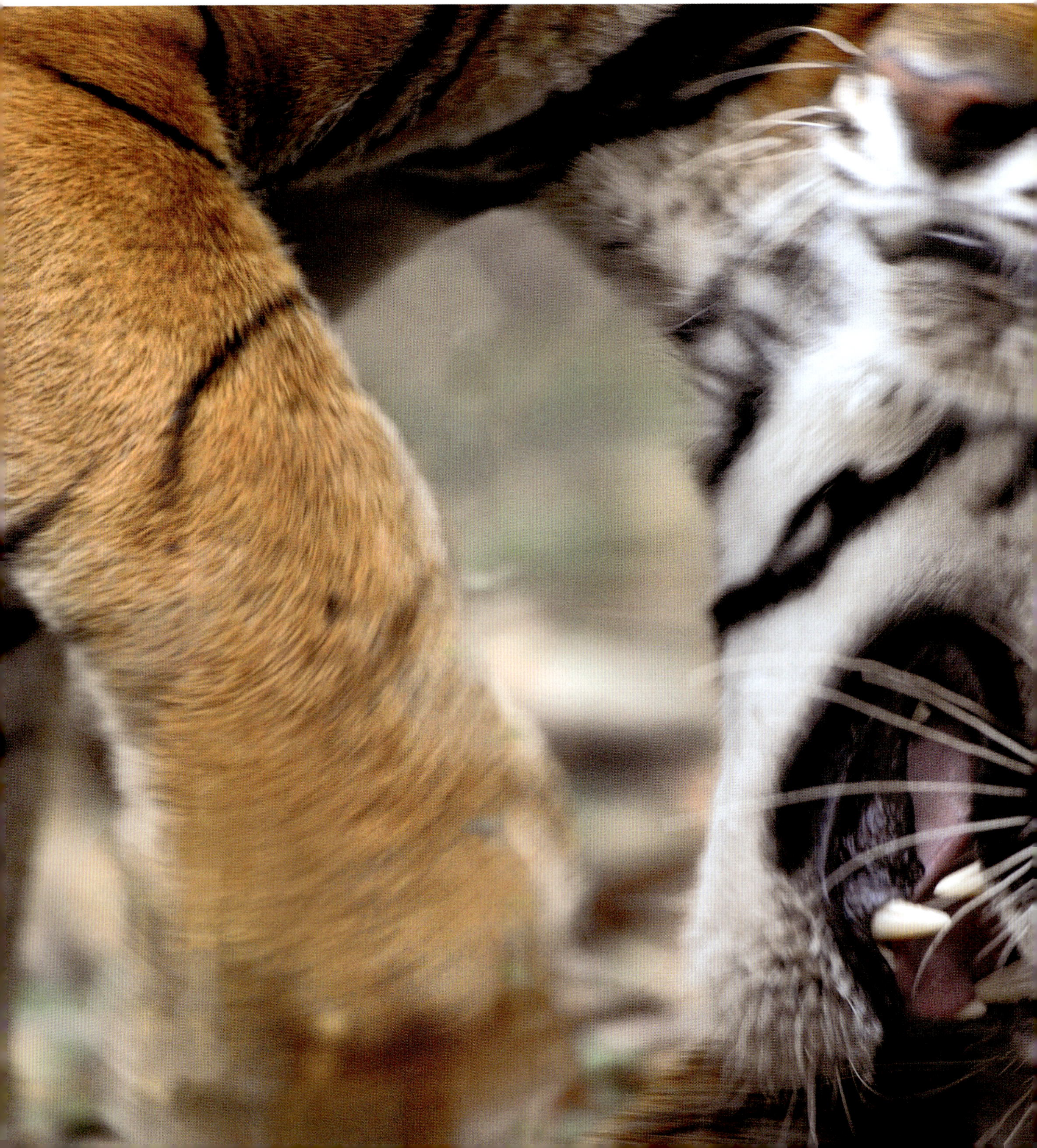

PRIVATE LIVES

As a solitary animal, a tiger needs special signals to show that it agrees to meet another of its kind. Obviously this is what happens when it is time to mate, but only if the female is receptive. When that moment comes, the nearest male quickly finds out about it, thanks to the distinctive scent that she produces in her urine.
To find out if a female is on heat, the male sniffs her urine and takes a little of it into his mouth. After savouring a few drops he makes an odd movement with his lips and puts out his tongue in a grimace that was called 'flehmen' by the German biologists who first described it.
This behaviour is not unique to the tigers: many other mammals use it too. Thus, the male takes a sample of the female's hormones in order to assess how receptive she is. This chemical analysis is carried out by an organ inside the mouth, at the front of the palate, and known as Jacobson's organ. The grimace may allow the animal to put the drops of liquid in contact with

Contact between males and females requires a certain amount of patience from both parties, who sometimes need to get to know each other. Their encounters may then seem intense, but they never last long – a few days at the very most – and may occur at any time of the year.

this organ. Primates, including humans, possess a rudimentary Jacobson's organ and it may be what we use when tasting wine! If the test result is positive, the male next tries to make contact with the female, calling to her, trying to get close and showing himself to her.

Mating sessions are marked by numerous couplings, in the course of which the male holds the female in position by grasping the back of her neck in his mouth. Judging from the sharp slap she gives him after their exertions, she does not always seem to appreciate this. The pair also communicate with sounds, making the whole jungle echo with their ardour.

However, even tigers have to be able to be patient in order to be accepted. If the animals have been neighbours for some time, the relationship may take shape more quickly and more peacefully than if they have never met. The tenderness that is noticeable when a male and female are surprised together doesn't always happen immediately. The first contact can be quite brutal, with the female sometimes taking some persuading before she accepts the presence of her suitor. Afterwards, mating is frenetic: anything from 17 to 52 couplings have been counted in a single 24-hour period!

It is also quite a spectacle: the male holds the female's neck in his mouth then, when the act is completed, he has to be careful to dodge the slap with outstretched claws that she gives him, growling, before rolling on her back. The presence of dermal spines on the penis, and the pain these must cause when the male withdraws, are probably the reason for this sudden aggression on the part of the female. In tigers, ovulation does not happen spontaneously in the course of the reproductive cycle: all this stimulation seems to be necessary to induce it and thus to ensure that the female becomes pregnant. For a few days the animals are inseparable. However, at the end of this brief period, the male returns to his bachelor existence, leaving the female to cope with pregnancy, birth and raising the young alone. The presence of such a dominant male, the father of the little tigers-to-be, is nevertheless essential.

Females seen in the wild may be accompanied by cubs of different sizes, but rarely very small ones, which they guard carefully against the jungle's many dangers (this page, top, and right). Observation of very small tiger cubs in captivity has shed light on various previously unknown aspects of their upbringing and growth (above).

Even if he has no further direct contact with the tigress, he provides security for the family, protecting it from incursions by other, possibly hostile males. But sometimes the whole family does get together again. A sight that surprised biologists was that of a female with cubs lying calmly in the company of a male, probably the father of her cubs, in a pool in Ranthambhore National Park in India on a very hot day. This observation confirmed that the degree to which males and young get on together depends a great deal on how closely they are related. The tiger's social life turns out to be much richer and more complex than we had imagined. The death of an adult male causes upsets in a tiger population. If the local protector disappears, another, often unknown, tiger rushes in to take over the newly vacated territory and those of the associated females.

This newcomer represents a real threat to the cubs

Because the male wants to reproduce, he will kill the cubs so that their mother will quickly come into season again and mate with him. Otherwise, this male, who may not yet have any descendants, will have to wait about two years until the tigress has raised her previous litter before he can sire his own. A tiger's reproductive life is quite short, an average of barely three years for a male, realistically six for a female. This explains why, in various species of mammal, adult males who have just taken over a group start by eliminating the young: it increases their chances of ensuring their own posterity. Sexually mature at three or four years, young females can have a litter every two years. At the end of the gestation period, which lasts 95-110 days, usually 103, they give birth to an average of three cubs. Newborns weigh anything from 0.8-1.6 kg (1¾-3½ lb). In comparison to a tigress of 100 kg (220 lb), and there are some a lot larger, the babies are tiny.

They are born with their eyes closed – they will open after 6-14 days – and possibly deaf. They grow quickly, quadrupling their birth weight in a month, thanks to the milk provided by their mother. A tiger has two pairs of teats on the abdomen, fewer than a domestic cat, which has four. The female gives birth in a safe hiding place – a dense thicket, the stump of a fallen tree, a rocky scree or a crevice – near a source of water and out of reach of the many predators who could be prowling around. For the first few days she doesn't leave her babies for an instant except to drink, but after that she has to hunt, to keep up her milk production and her own fitness. With tigers the choice of place and time to give birth comes from a thorough knowledge of nature's cycles, of the area in which they live and a perfect understanding on the part of each female of her individual territory. In Siberia, cubs are born in spring. In the other areas where tigers still live – which are all in tropical and subtropical zones – reproduction doesn't depend on the seasons and cubs may be seen almost all year round.

By the time they are a few weeks old, tiger cubs can chew on meat that their mother brings back to them

They play with their food and discover new scents and new tastes. Weaning takes place gradually from three to nine months; the female must hunt intensively because the cubs have hearty appetites.

A tigress being followed by offspring who are nearing the age of independence is a sign of hope, even though as far as the youngsters are concerned the most difficult challenge is yet to come: coping alone. Once her cubs reach this age, a female may come into season and become pregnant again, which accelerates the process of separation from her previous litter.

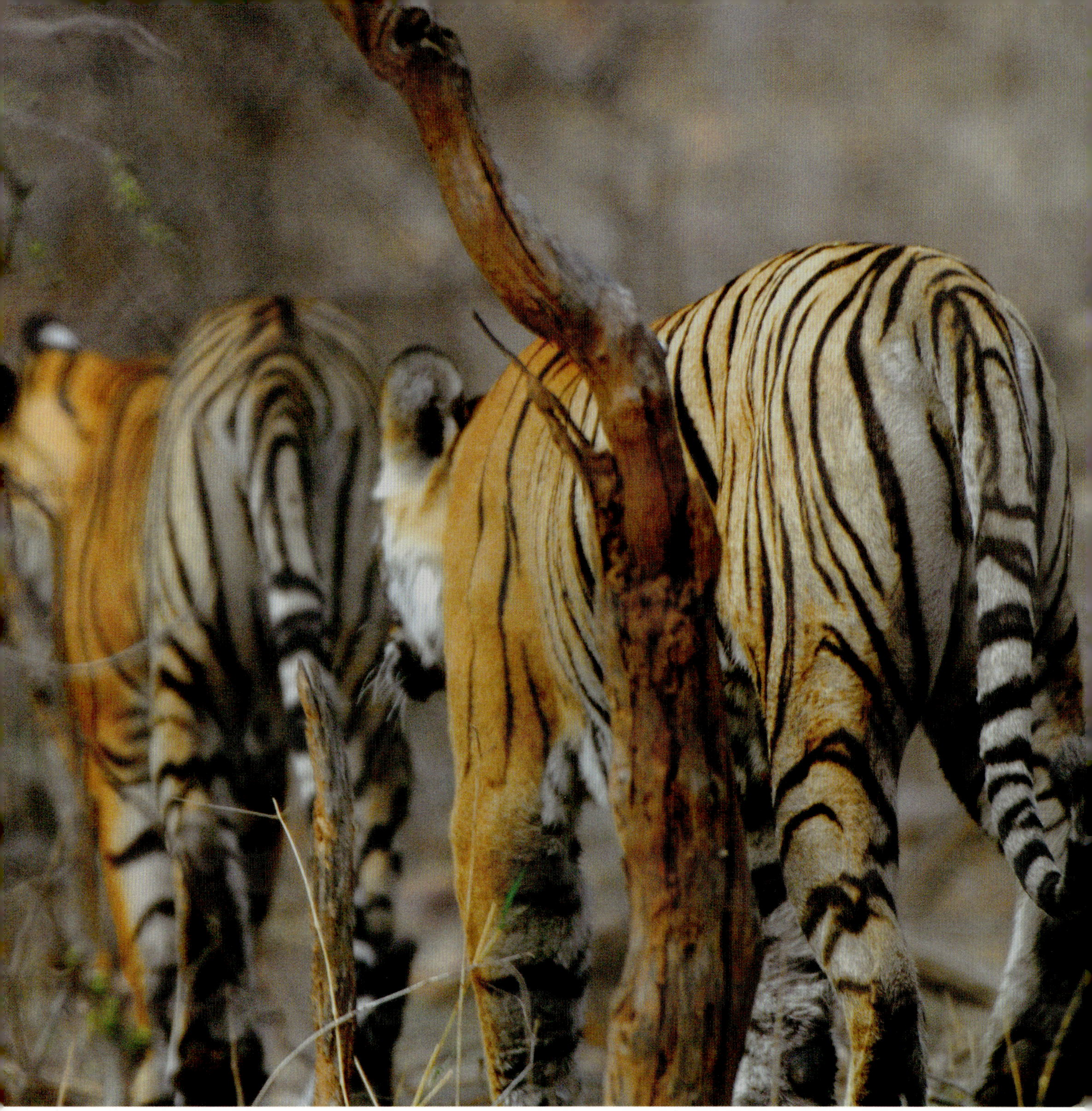

By the time they are ready to leave their mother, the youngsters are almost as large as she is. During their last moments together, they still exchange many signs of affection. A few weeks from now, the young female may well establish herself in the vicinity of her natal range, while her brother sets out in search of a territory farther away.

She may take a wide range of prey and it is possible that the cubs' future tastes are partly connected to what she introduces them to at this time. They begin to scamper after her at five or six months, a little before they are fully weaned and at the beginning of their real education, which lasts almost 18 months. Accompanying their mother when she hunts, watching her, working out how to control their strength and their youthful enthusiasm, using all their senses advisedly, the little tigers learn to be grown-ups.

Finding an approachable prey, neither too heavy nor too dangerous, stalking close to it without being seen, grabbing hold of it, killing it: nothing is easy. Little more than half of all tigers live to be more than two years old. Watching a female followed by large cubs is impressive. It is also a sign of hope for the species and of success for the mother, who has managed to bring them this far, close to the point of independence. But it is also a fragile symbol, because at this age the youngsters' chances of survival are still so remote. Natural selection knows no uncertainties. In addition to purring when they are little, a tigress has several ways of communicating with her cubs. There is the 'summons' call she uses when she returns to the hiding place where they are waiting for her, the cry she emits to tell them to join her once the hunt is over when they have been following at a distance, and an alarm signal when they need to hide. Tigers also communicate visually over short distances. The white spots on the back

Although their upbringing has been identical, the two adolescent tigers (opposite) will henceforth take very different paths through life. Once they have separated they will probably not see each other again, though the young female may continue to have a certain amount of contact with her mother (this page).

of the black ears are good signals when the female is moving through the undergrowth, accompanied by her young. A tigress's first hunts with her offspring hot on her heels are pretty irritating. Usually she instructs them to stay behind so that she can capture the chosen prey on her own, without them getting in the way. Observation is also an effective way of learning. Afterwards the youngsters come to join their mother for dinner. It's easier for several tigers together to defend their kill against anyone who comes to bother them; on the other hand the leftovers won't last as long when there are more mouths to feed. The young can join in the hunting properly only when their four adult canines come through, at between 12 and 18 months. First attempts at hunting are often risky. The juveniles are not good at judging distance, don't focus on their victim properly or don't choose it judiciously enough. If there are two or three of them, however, even a poorly co-ordinated attack makes up in strength in numbers what the individual effort still lacks. Young males become independent more quickly and need to learn to get by on their own sooner than their sisters.

The fact that young males move some distance away after they have achieved independence allows for an intermingling of genes in a population by separating closely related individuals. This and the fact that adults have quite a short reproductive life help to prevent inbreeding.

So they practise on any available prey. They still have to be careful not to attack an Indian porcupine *(Hystrix indica)* or its Malay cousin *(H. brachyura)* before they know what they are doing, though both species are regular items on an adult's menu. There have been several reports of tigers being killed when crossing the territory of other, established adults. A tiger without a territory is an animal in danger, under a suspended sentence, and with no chance of reproducing. When tiger populations occupy extensive areas, the rhythm of natural renewal allows the subadults to find some available space. A young male may travel dozens of kilometres before finding a territory, but nowadays that happens more and more rarely, because the reserves are surrounded by stretches of land hostile to the big cat, whether they be farmland or built-up areas. If it comes

Males need huge ranges, and those who are already established hold on tight to their piece of jungle

to a conflict, an animal defending its territory generally has the advantage over one that is trying to take it over. Resident tigers have no hesitation in killing impatient youngsters who dare to challenge them. In this scenario, animals have no time to grow old – before that happens they are eliminated by younger and fitter rivals. This is why animals in captivity may live longer than those living freely in the wild. Young females are perhaps a little luckier. If their mother's territory is spacious and well stocked, they can set up home in part of it, tolerated by her and accepted by the local resident male or males. When their mother disappears, they will more or less take over her domain. In tiger society, females are more sedentary than males, sometimes moving as little as 10 km (6 miles).

in failed attacks on this large rodent. Either the wounds inflicted by the porcupine's spines have been fatal, or the after-effects have made the big cat unable to hunt, condemning it to die of hunger. Young males who have just become independent are the most exposed to the hazards of life, particularly

Tigers' explorations – particularly those of males, when all the territories near their birthplace are taken – explain why individuals are regularly seen far from their permanent places of residence. In past centuries and up to the beginning of the 20th, reliable data reported sightings and captures of Caspian tigers *(P. t. virgata)* in central Siberia, well north of the subspecies' known permanent range. This natural behaviour shows that, if places favourable to the tiger still exist and if populations remain viable and continue to grow, it should be possible to repopulate the former from the latter, one piece of land at a time. The males would come first, followed by the females. During the youngsters' long period of dependence on their mother, she shows them great patience and affection. As soon as they leave the den where they were born, scenes of rest and relaxation in the open air reveal some lovely aspects of family life. As befits their age, the little ones seem carefree, while the tigress is often trying to recover from

A tigress with her family, a brother and sister together, sharing a peaceful siesta – there is so much hope for future generations of tigers in the Indian parks. But if these prospects are to continue, the wild spaces must remain welcoming and provide enough food. The basics of the problem are well known; what we need to do is draw the right conclusions.

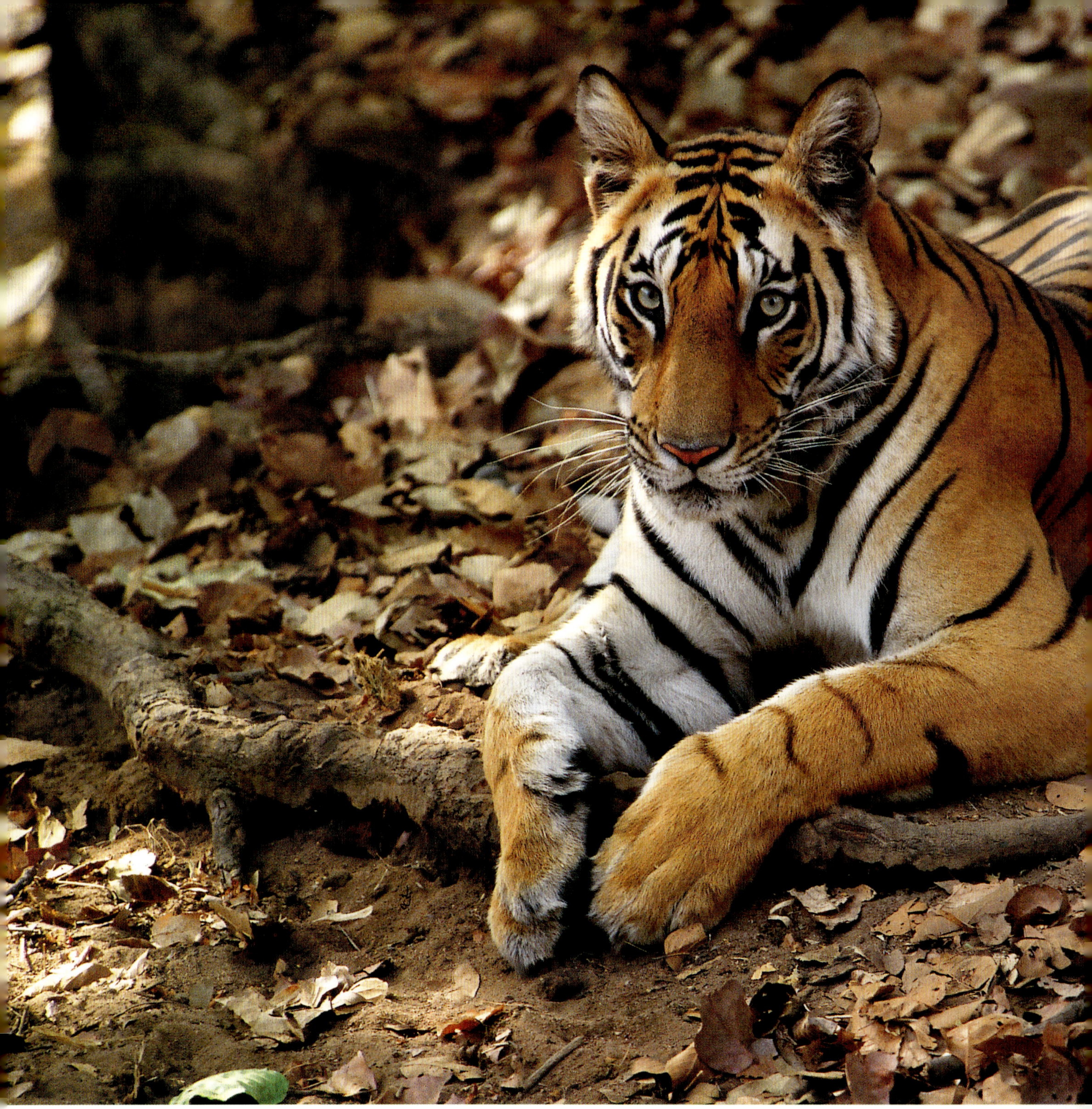

one exhausting hunt before setting out on another. If there are several cubs, they spend a lot of time together, although this doesn't stop them often wanting to draw their mother into their exercises and pranks. The jerky movements of the end of her tail, in particular, provide the opportunity to practise leaping on prey. Licking is an important activity for tigers. A tiger's tongue, like that of all cats, is covered with horny papillae that make it very rasping. This is useful for licking the skin of a kill and almost enough to open it up when the prey is small. We can only imagine the effect of a tigress licking the muzzle of one of her babies. It is certainly invigorating and apparently very effective at stimulating them. It is also good at cleaning up a muzzle that is red with blood after a meal. The animals also lick each other, ridding their coats of any remains that could attract insects and getting rid of parasites. Some tiger habitats are hard to access and do not make field studies easy. But when these difficulties are removed, we discover how varied tiger behaviour can be.

Learning to be independent and acquiring a territory are critical stages in a tiger's life, as this young female, who has just separated from her mother and still looks quite immature, is finding out.

Despite its reputation as a solitary creature, the Asian big cat has a rich and complex social life

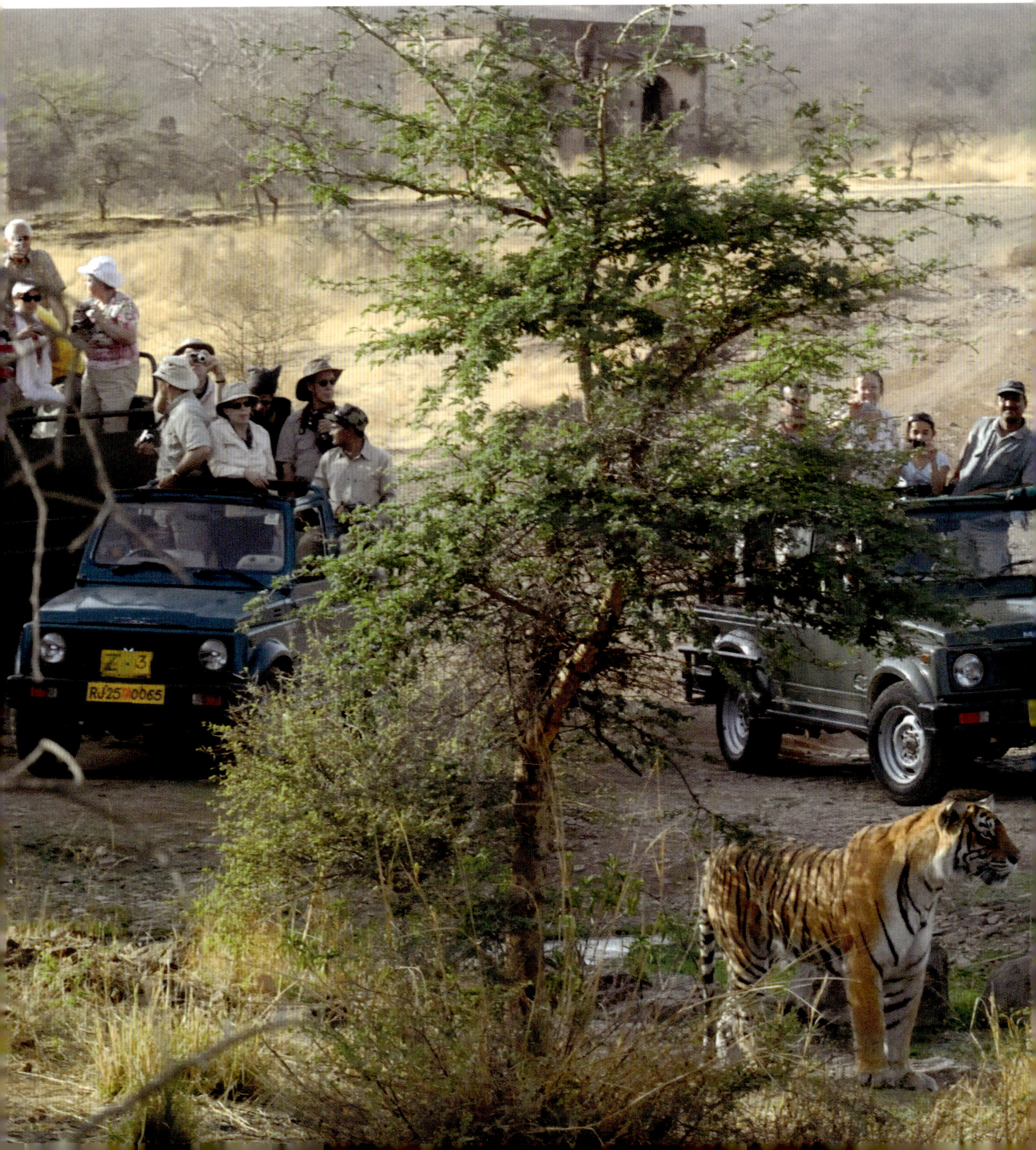

OF TIGERS AND MEN

At the end of the 19th century tiger hunts often took place on elephant back, as this engraving from 1867 shows. The black and white photo, taken from the archives of the gunsmiths Holland and Holland, shows how heavily tigers were hunted until the mid-20th century. As for the tigress, her flattened ears bear witness to her anxiety, caused by the unconscious harassment of over-eager visitors.

In the arts, stories and legends, traditions and religions, tigers have survived in numerous parts of Asia where in reality they are now extinct. The oldest objects on which they appear date back 5,000 years in the form of figurines or engravings on seals from the Indus civilisation (modern-day Pakistan). More recently, the tiger joined the pantheon of Hindu gods, especially after the Aryans reached what is now India. A relationship between humans and tigers, fraught with ambiguity and paradox, persists in numerous Asian stories and contemporary practices. Today, it's on the borders of Europe that the historical documentation seems the most surprising. We know from writings and certain mosaics that the ancient Greeks and Romans were familiar with tigers. These would have come from Anatolia and Persia and belonged to the Caspian subspecies *(P. t. virgata)*, previously known as the Hyrcanian tiger

(Hyrcania was the ancient name for the land on the south-east coast of the Black Sea). The French botanist Joseph Pitton de Tournefort (1656-1708) wrote an *Account of a Journey to the Levant* in 1700-1702 in which he describes an encounter with tigers at the foot of Mount Ararat (in Anatolia, eastern Turkey): *'The tigers that we caught sight of were none the less frightening for being more than a hundred paces from us, nor for our being assured that they were not in the habit of coming to insult passers-by.'* The Hyrcan tiger is mentioned in Shakespeare's *Macbeth*, and in *Songs of Experience* the poet William Blake (1757-1827) famously wrote:
Tyger, tyger, burning bright
In the forests of the night...
Tigers have been a source of inspiration well beyond the lands where they have ever lived. The traditions have certainly outlasted the

Like many celebrated animals tigers were respected and hunted at the same time

species that gave birth to them. To kill a tiger in single combat was seen as an act of courage, and legends peddling such stories quickly sprouted. Many Asian myths pay homage to solitary heroes who killed tigers in Homeric struggles. The reasons were classic: to protect domestic flocks in areas where wildlife had been decimated, to procure a magnificent pelt and – already – to use the tiger's organs in traditional medicine. The prestige conferred by a tiger-skin garment dates back to antiquity and endures to this day. So-called 'game' hunting was mostly practised in India, at the period of the maharajahs and the British Raj. The hunters rode elephants, while beaters on foot forced the big cats towards them.

"The tiger appears in monastery paintings and cultural artefacts in Tibet, but using tiger skins to trim festive garments was traditionally the privilege of chieftains and army generals. It was only in the late 1990s and early 2000s that tiger skins became popular as a fashion statement during festivals. When the connection between the slaughter of wild tigers in India and the skins for sale in the streets of Lhasa was pointed out by the Dalai Lama and a huge public awareness campaign, the people of Tibet soon curbed their use. Those tiger skins were all smuggled from India, killed by poachers, as the tiger-breeding farms in China cannot legally sell skins, bones or other tiger body parts. China has stiff laws against the illegal wildlife trade and the smuggling of tiger parts across its borders. But any law is only as effective as its implementation. I think China can do a lot more to help secure a future for wild tigers; by sending a clear message across the world that it is serious about maintaining its ban on the use of tiger bone in TCM; by closing down its tiger farms; by destroying its stockpiles of tiger parts; by improving enforcement; and by sending a strong message to Chinese consumers."
Belinda Wright, Executive Director, Wildlife Protection Society of India

Photos of the period show that a single day's hunting could result in the death of several tigers. Some maharajahs tried to limit the shooting, but not all foreign officials respected such restrictions. Some hunters could boast of having accounted for hundreds of tigers in their lifetime. Figures that survive from this period bear witness to the wealth of wildlife that existed over the last two centuries and go some way towards explaining the current decline. Some old, badly preserved, black and white snapshots are all that remain of the Balinese and the Caspian tigers. Nowadays, hunting involves four-wheel-drive vehicles, mobile phones, GPS and automatic weapons, which are unfortunately numerous in too many parts of the world – including Asia. Poaching persists, using traditional equipment as well as modern methods: the financial incentives are just too strong. Yes, protected areas have been created in an effort to save the tiger. But the protection is often more effective on paper than it is on the ground. There is all sorts of pressure on the forests – the need to find new agricultural land, or to develop new industrial or residential areas. From Iran to the extreme east of Russia, there nevertheless exist protected areas where tigers are still found, or were until quite recently. Established in the 1970s, one of the most structured networks of reserves is in India. These tiger reserves have had varying degrees of success and, in 2004, some grave mismanagement was revealed. Some of the reserves had very few tigers left and others, such as Sariska, none at all. The animals had all disappeared without anyone noticing – at least officially. So serious reassessment of tiger conservation is necessary. There are probably no more than a few hundred wild tigers left in all India, realistically no more than 1,500 in 2008, compared with more than 3,600 in 2001-2002. In places where tigers still exist and there are reception facilities, you can visit these reserves in the hope of seeing them, just as you would the rest of the flora and fauna.

This 19th-century miniature (above left) bears witness to the fact that Indian literature abounds with stories and pictures of tiger hunting. Human pressure on protected areas – above at the time of the pilgrimage for the god Ganesh in Ranthambhore National Park – can disturb both plants and animals. Nevertheless, accidents involving people are very rare. The big cat has to find places well away from human activity, where it can live its life in peace.

101

Wildlife-based tourism can be a good thing. Some of India's national parks offer the opportunity to approach tigers on elephant back, which seems more respectful of the animals than the floods of vehicles jam-packed with visitors that sometimes converge on them. Perhaps we should ask the tigers what they think...

This gives rise to scenarios that speak volumes: perhaps ten vehicles crowd round a tiger which is trying to slip away discreetly or is resting too close to a track. Elephant-back safaris are a more appropriate approach to tiger viewing and have been developed particularly in Bandhavgarh and Kahna in Madhya Pradesh, in Corbett in Uttarakhand, and in Mudumalai and Bandipur in southern India. A study method much used in recent years is that of installing photographic traps in areas where tigers are thought to live and where we would like to know if there are any left. Judiciously placed, these devices can

Eco-tourism should not result in the harassment of wildlife, and particularly not of tigers

identify quite a lot of members of the local fauna and sometimes bring pleasant surprises such as the discovery of an unexpected animal. They have also been known to take photos of poachers! Individual tigers can be distinguished by their unique patterns of stripes and markings. With the help of calculations taking account of the area being monitored, the number of cameras used, the length of time the traps are in place and other parameters such as the number of different individuals identified and the number of times the same animal is photographed, an estimate of the size of the local population can be made. Other study methods 'in the field' include finding paw prints, which are sometimes sufficient to distinguish individuals in a small area.

An unappealing task that can nevertheless yield a great deal of information is collecting tiger dung: a researcher has to be able to recognise this, then analyse the remains of the prey the tiger has eaten. This is one of the best ways of studying a species' diet. As a result we know that in Nagarhole

National Park in southern India, the average weight of captured animals, calculated on the basis of bodies that have been recovered, is close to 400 kg (900 lb), while that of the prey identified in excrement is only 91 kg (200 lb). That indicates that tigers eat numerous small kills of which no remains are found. In the depths of the jungle, it is easier to find the bones of a gaur than those of a porcupine! Another method, regarded as 'invasive', necessitates capturing animals, anaesthetising them and fitting

It is essential that studies of tiger biology continue, as our current knowledge is so fragmented. Some methods are considered invasive, as they involve capturing the cats in order to fit them with radio collars. In other cases, it is enough to follow their footprints or to take plaster casts.

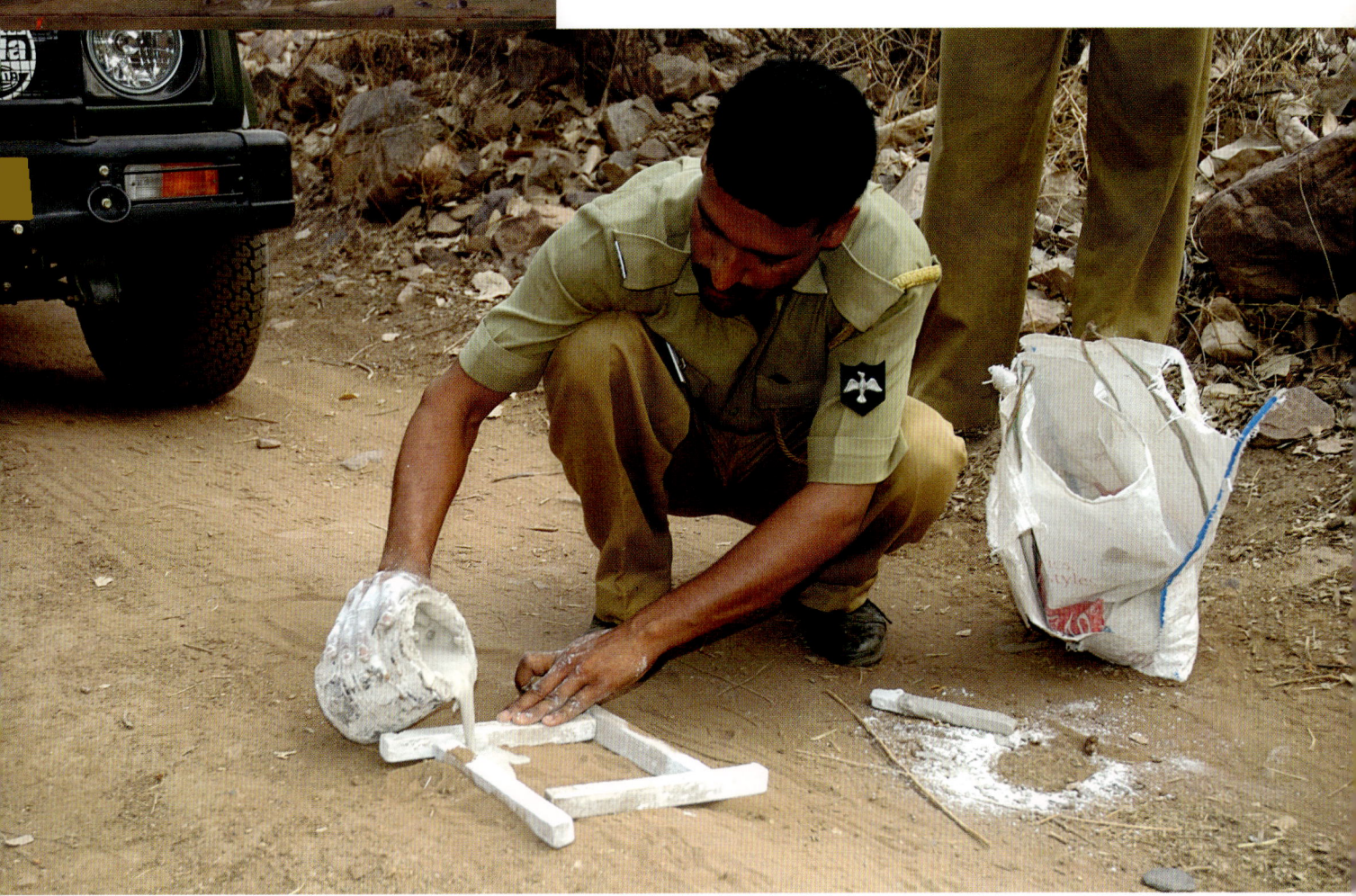

105

them with a radio collar. They are then released and, thanks to some tall aerials, can be followed on foot, by car, on elephant back, even from a light aircraft or via satellite. Using triangulation, it is possible to mark on a map where a tiger was at the time of contact. This enables us to determine the limits of the territories of the animals being studied, their patterns of activity and the areas they cover. On the other hand, it is important not to confuse nature reserves where tigers live freely with tiger farms. More than 5,000 tigers live in about 200 farms in China, probably more than are living in the wild across their entire range. Above and beyond the fact that the way these big cats are kept is not conducive to their reintroduction into the wild, it is not clear where they came from. They are reared for use in traditional Asian medicine, which poses the most serious threat to the species, the paradox being that a bone from a wild tiger commands a higher price than one from a farmed tiger. So the farms do not help to stamp out poaching – quite the reverse. Add this to the threats posed by habitat destruction and the outcome could be fatal for the species.

For all the haughty pose and the noble bearing of an invincible animal, this tigress's future is in our hands. We must all try to find answers to the question of how to preserve the tiger and the eco-systems in which it lives, while still being mindful of the needs of the men and women who share those areas.

The demand for tiger-based products is mind-blowing!

A number of cultures attribute certain properties to various plants and animals, and people convince themselves that by eating them they will acquire the same qualities. All you need to do is believe it!

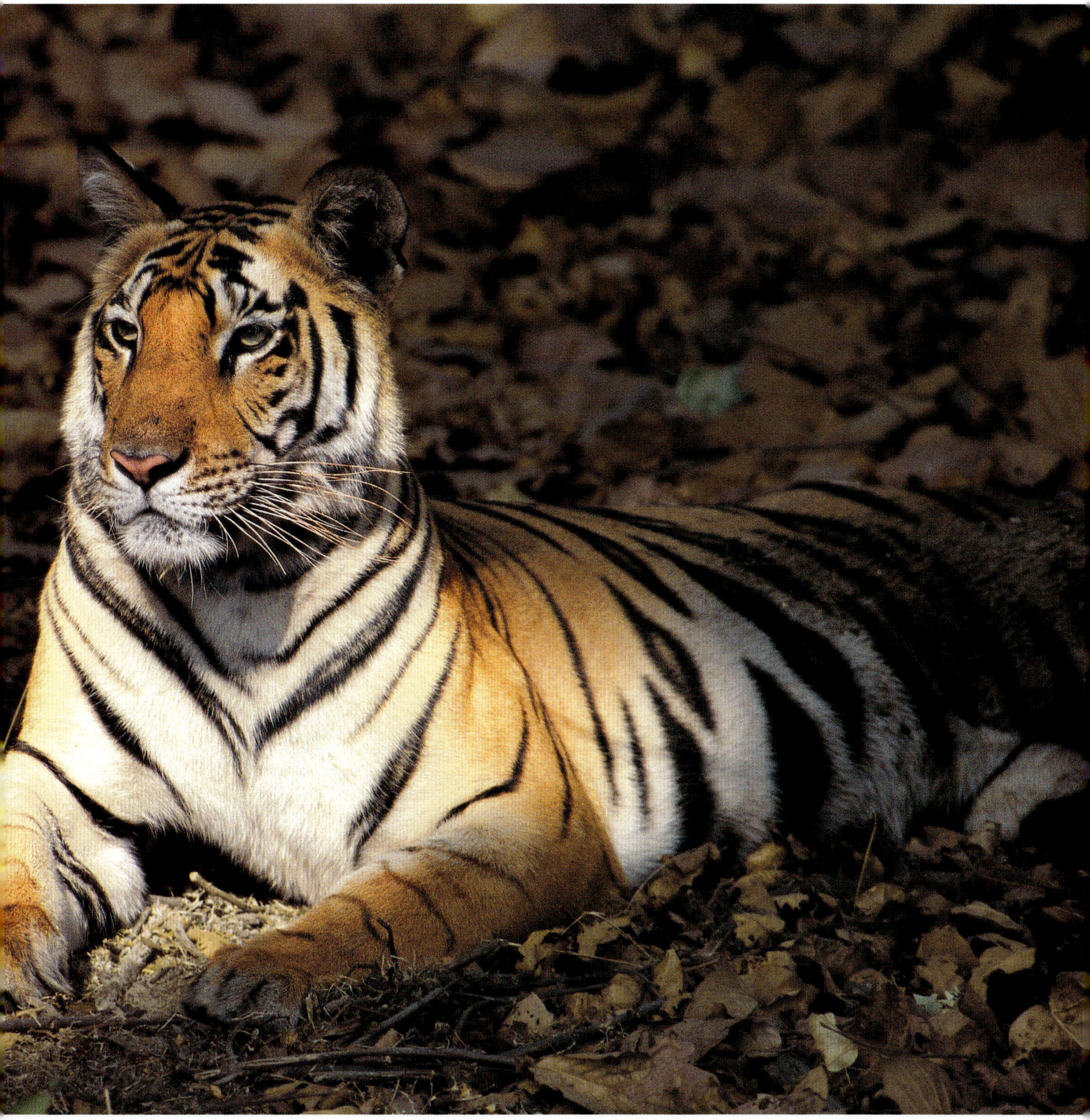

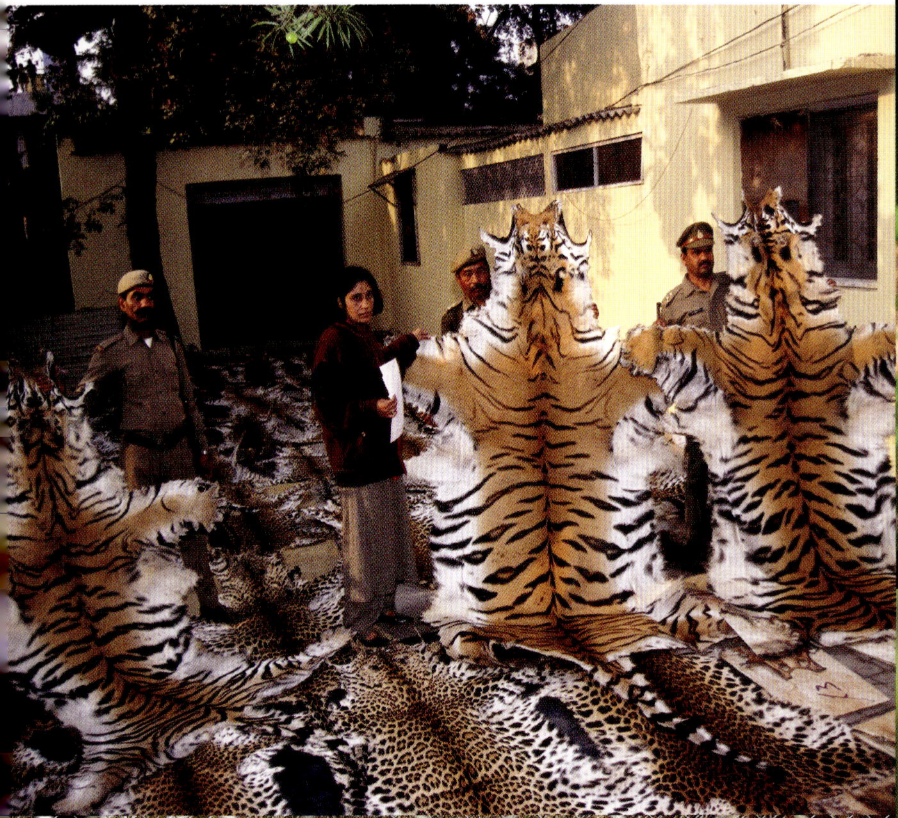

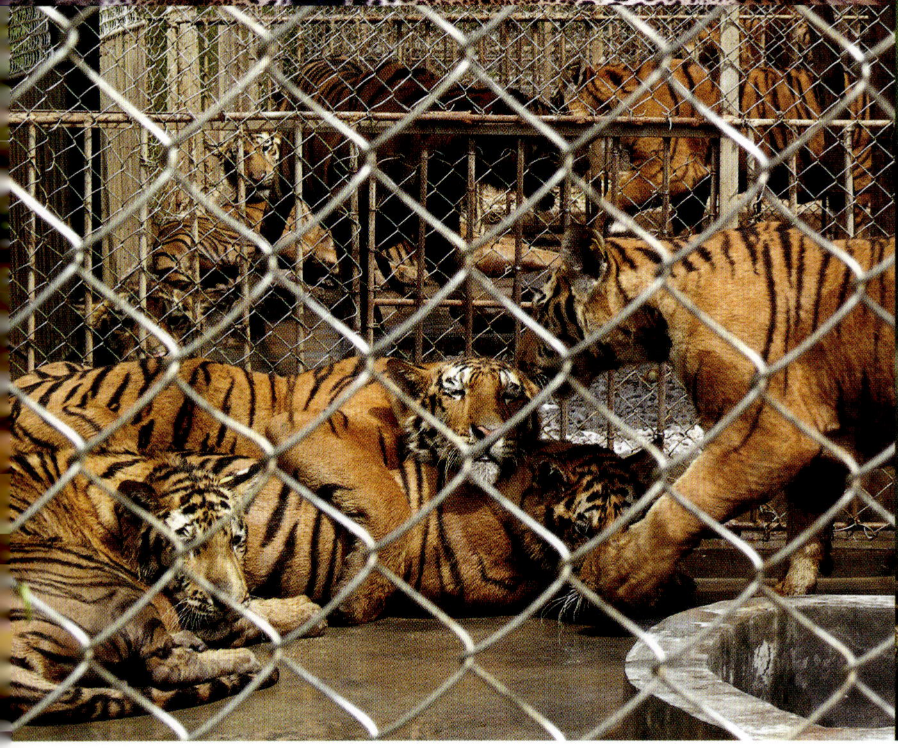

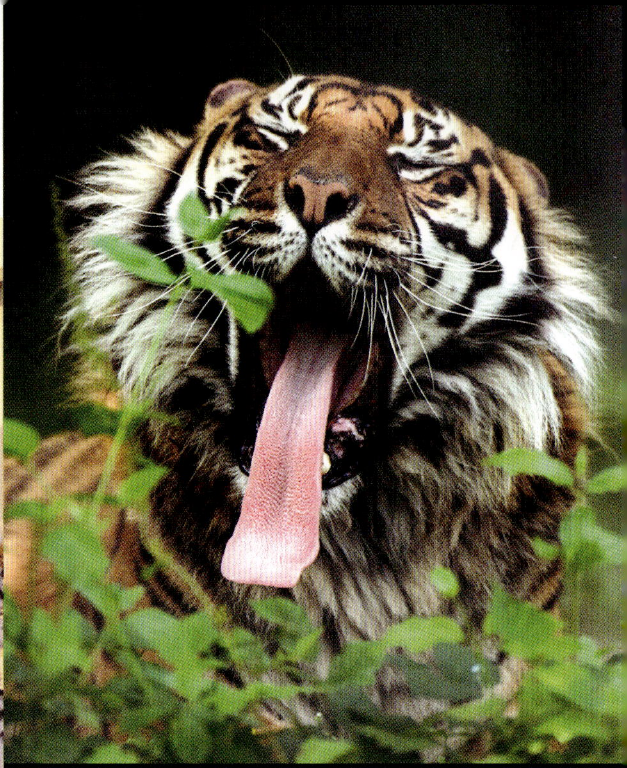

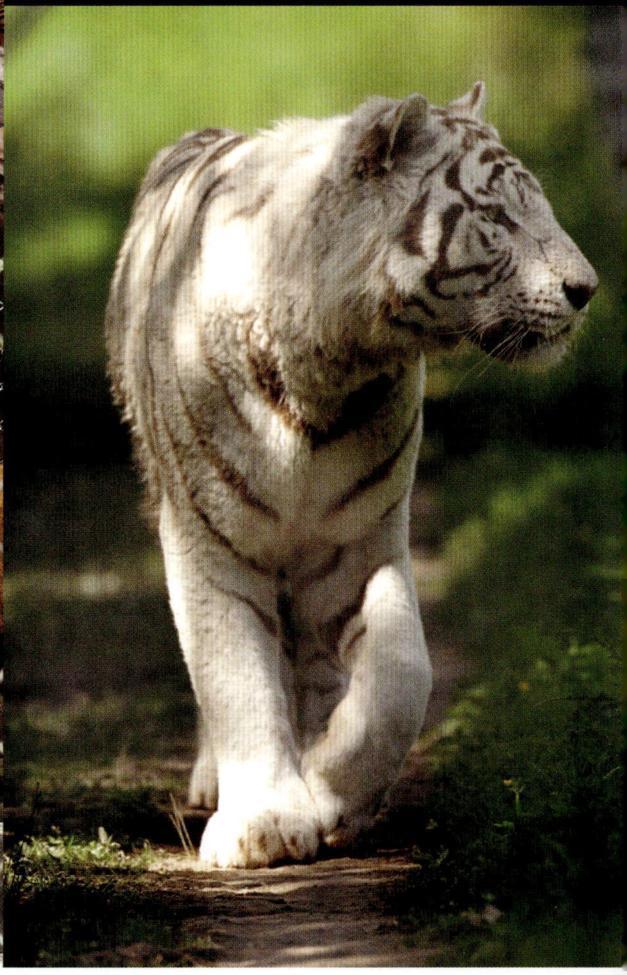

In the traditional Chinese pharmacopoeia, the tiger in all its forms is endowed with innumerable virtues which guarantee a lot of money to those who trade in it. At the beginning of the 21st century there are probably no wild tigers left in China, although there were once five subspecies *(P. t. tigris, P. t. amoyensis, P. t. altaica, P. t. virgata* and *P. t. corbetti),* all of which have been eradicated. The most famous tiger product is called Os tigris – tiger bone. Classed as a 'herb' in traditional Chinese medicine (TCM), it is prescribed for rheumatism, muscle weakness, stiffness and lumbar pain.

The powdered bone is mixed with plants such as amaranthus and angelica, and taken as a wine or a pill. Every bit of the tiger is good, every bit can be sold and all of Asia buys it, from India to Korea, China to Indonesia: the fat to protect against leprosy, the claws as a sedative, the penis as an aphrodisiac, the tail to treat skin diseases, the eyes to treat cataracts, the humerus for rheumatism. The quantities traded are significant. In 1993 almost 500 kg (1,100 lb) of tiger bone were seized in India in a single haul, and the quantity imported into South Korea between 1970 and 1993 is estimated at 9 tonnes (almost 40,000 lb). One can only imagine how many animals have been killed as a result. But the big cat sometimes takes its revenge: man-eating tigers are not unknown. Among the many accounts of their misdeeds, those of Jim Corbett (1875–1955), published as *Man-eaters of Kumaon* in 1944, are the best known. Born in the north of India, Corbett lived there until independence in 1947. An expert on Indian wildlife, he first hunted it, then rapidly became one of its most ardent defenders, as his works show.

In the Himalayan foothills of Uttarakhand there is a national park which bears his name. The rare phenomenon of man-eating tigers is a different matter from the accidental attacks which happen occasionally anywhere that tigers live. A wounded animal can be dangerous, as can a female with cubs who thinks that her young are under threat.

Today there are more tigers in captivity than there are in the wild, and who knows how many are killed each year? Chinese 'tiger farms' (bottom left) do not prevent poaching, which is still rife, as this display of confiscated skins shows. Nowadays most zoos serve the valuable function of increasing public awareness; tigers such as the Sumatran (above) can be ambassadors for their cause, as long as they send out the right messages to educate visitors.

109

When out for a walk in tiger country, it is better to avoid these individuals than to take them by surprise. The Sundarban tigers are a special case. This region, where forests, sea inlets and rivers intertwine, is used by foresters and fisherfolk who come to cut wood, gather honey and stretch out fishing nets. Between 1984 and 2006, tiger attacks were regularly recorded. In Bangladesh 495 people were killed. Several ways of guarding against a tiger attack have been developed. Visitors wear a mask on the back of the neck and, as tigers generally pounce on their prey from behind, they are fooled by this second face, which appears to be watching them, and refrain from attacking. Mannequins tied to an electric battery are also positioned close to human encampments. Tigers that attack them suffer an electric shock and the hope is that they will associate the pain with any subsequent attack. Finally, dogs have been brought into the equation, because, with their superior sense of smell, they detect wildlife, including tigers, before humans do. Demographic pressure, poaching, loss of habitat… The threats to the tiger are numerous, but it is not acceptable that it might die out. It can never be acceptable for a species to die out.

Human activity inside or on the fringes of protected areas must not be allowed to interfere with the parks' aims. Fishing or foraging with elephants in Kaziranga, burning vegetation in Corbett all seem to be more intrusive than one might wish. But what alternative can we offer the people concerned?

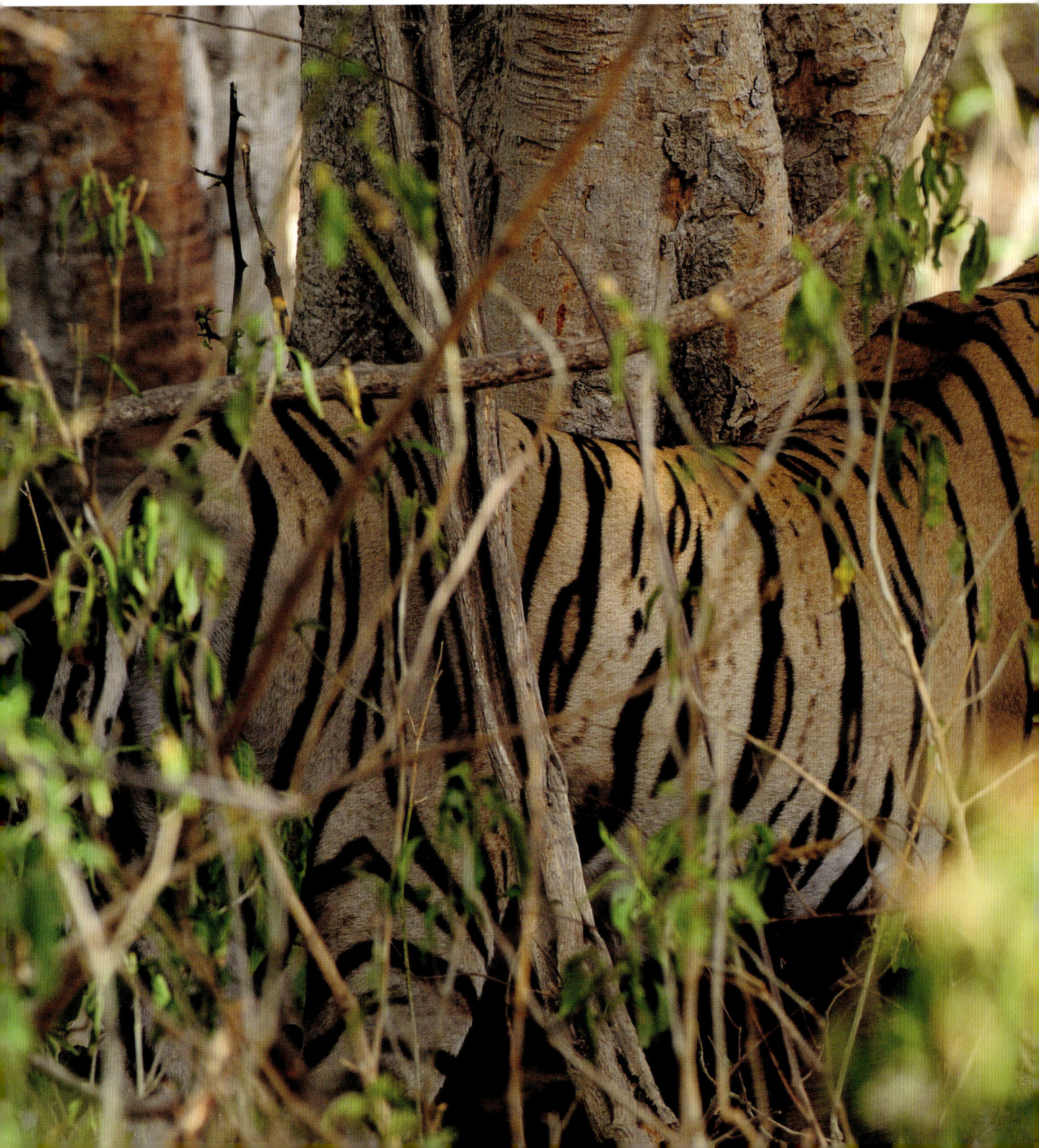

THE UNWRITTEN FUTURE

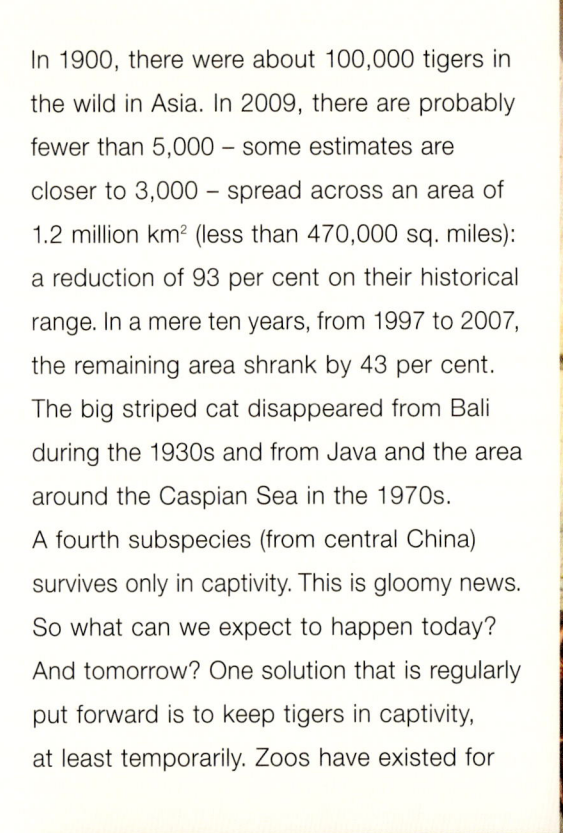

In 1900, there were about 100,000 tigers in the wild in Asia. In 2009, there are probably fewer than 5,000 – some estimates are closer to 3,000 – spread across an area of 1.2 million km^2 (less than 470,000 sq. miles): a reduction of 93 per cent on their historical range. In a mere ten years, from 1997 to 2007, the remaining area shrank by 43 per cent. The big striped cat disappeared from Bali during the 1930s and from Java and the area around the Caspian Sea in the 1970s. A fourth subspecies (from central China) survives only in captivity. This is gloomy news. So what can we expect to happen today? And tomorrow? One solution that is regularly put forward is to keep tigers in captivity, at least temporarily. Zoos have existed for

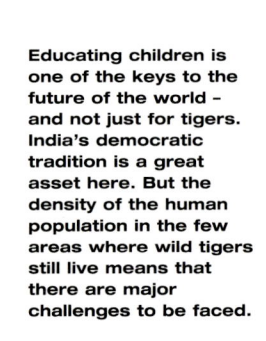

Educating children is one of the keys to the future of the world – and not just for tigers. India's democratic tradition is a great asset here. But the density of the human population in the few areas where wild tigers still live means that there are major challenges to be faced.

a long time, and some of them have been exhibiting tigers for just as long. Tigers do quite well in captivity and reproduce easily. Nowadays, there are more tigers in captivity around the world than there are in the wild in Asia. It is estimated that there are 11,000 in captivity, of which 5,000 are in Chinese farms. A ray of hope for the species? That remains to be seen. Many of these cats are bought and sold on, moved from one park to another, their exact place of origin forgotten. Thus a Siberian tiger may mate with one from Bengal, but the offspring is not the same as an individual from a wild population.

Yes, the majority of tigers in zoos serve to heighten public awareness of the species' problems in their countries of origin, but this can never replace lost wild populations. That said, it can prevent the capture of further wild individuals and spread the word about the continual mismanagement of the environment and its biodiversity. Being able to breed animals in captivity in order to release them into the wild is the hope of many zoos. But few have succeeded. A young tiger has to know its forest if it is to have any chance of taking over a territory. It must learn to hunt, which means identifying prey and knowing how to stalk and kill it – skills which its mother teaches it in natural circumstances, but which are difficult to pass on behind bars. So it is fundamental to the tiger's survival that large enough wild spaces supporting sufficient prey remain.

Tigers are also among the stars of the circus. Is this necessary?

Some breeders have also played at crossing tigers with lions. The offspring are almost always sterile – so what is the point? And what about white tigers? A 1959 census in India counted at least 35, most of them adults and many of them having been killed by hunting parties. The unusual coat colour, probably linked to a mutation that appeared in the region about a hundred years ago, doesn't seem to compromise the animal's viability. The first white tiger to be captured alive – in 1951, in the forests of the former state of Rewa, where its mother and three siblings were killed at the same time – was placed in the park belonging to the palace of the Maharajah of Govindgarh. The animal, a young male aged about nine months, was subsequently raised in captivity and mated with a normally coloured female. All the resulting cubs had their mother's colouring. The same male was then mated to one of his daughters, giving the world four white tiger cubs. Noticeably larger than other tigers, these animals have a white coat with ash-coloured stripes, but they are not completely lacking in pigmentation and they are not albinos: their eyes are not red but blue. Since this natural mutation was fixed about 50 years ago, white tigers have turned up in a number of zoos. This is a paradoxical step, because concern for the species does not lie in the rather trivial question of whether or not to perpetuate a white-coated form, but rather in the conservation of habitats and wild populations. Sometimes, commercial interests seem to take precedence over scientific ones. So, the real question concerns the survival of the tiger in the wild, and reports from the ground are not reassuring. The establishment of Project Tiger in the 1970s seemed to formalise a real, global will to take positive action after decades of destruction. Although this involved only one country, it was a model for everyone trying to protect the tiger, an 'umbrella' species at the top of the ecological pyramid, a perfect symbol of what was at stake when it came to protecting the world's wildlife.

The high market value of white tigers is a mixed blessing born of the selective breeding of captive tigers. Known in India for decades, the mutation of the coat is of no value to the survival of the species. All the world's white tigers are descended from a young male who was captured and then mated with one of his daughters.

In the 1990s, the brutal revelations of extensive degradation came as a shock to many. Animals and habitats had quite simply disappeared. The monitoring of reserves turned out to be at the very least inappropriate. The economic explosion of the 1980s had a detrimental effect on the environment, with pressure from the human population increasing tenfold, particularly in Asia. Deforestation led to water shortages and soil erosion everywhere. The loss of nature reserves hasn't solved the immediate problems of survival for the people who are most directly involved. Preserving tigers and their forests also protects villages, cultures

and cattle. Preserving natural vegetation prevents water run-off and the breaking up of soil, and maintains water reserves.
So the networks of wildlife reserves and the 'corridors' that enable them to communicate with each other must be re-established as a matter of urgency. When reserves are isolated, animals cannot mix and the risk of extinction increases. Is it necessary to use legislation as a means of protecting the tiger and the environment? Of course it is. There are many national and international laws aimed at protecting them, but to date they have not prevented anything, because they have been inadequately or badly enforced. The tiger has been protected in Iran only since 1957, although it disappeared from there in 1953; not until 2004 was it removed from Turkey's list of vermin, decades after it was last seen. Russia, India and China have officially protected it for some decades, with the variable results that we know about. The main difficulty that must be sorted out urgently is the enforcement of the laws. Now, at the start of the 21st century, a new awareness is emerging of the need to try to save the tiger, which is in real danger of extinction in the wild. Projects flourish, but it is imperative that they be better administered than their predecessors.
The most westerly surviving tiger population lives in the north-west of India, in Rajaji National Park. The Chilla-Motichur corridor, linking Rajaji with Corbett National Park, must be re-established in order to improve the chances of survival of two populations which are currently isolated, with no possibility of interbreeding.
On 30 January 2008 it was decided to create an 8,000-km (5,000-mile) 'genetic corridor' connecting the tigers of Bhutan to those of Myanmar, with the possibility of an extension into South-east Asia as far as Vietnam. The dozen countries where free tigers survive must be allocated new funds earmarked for protected areas. The Western Ghats Reserve in India, the sanctuary of Kha Khaeng in Thailand, Taman Negara National Park in Malaysia and the Sikhote-Alin Reserve in Russia all offer good prospects of saving the tiger. An opportunity is also arising in the Indian reserve of Sariska.

Keeping animals in captivity is often mentioned as a way of saving endangered species. But experience has shown that this is not always successful. Some behaviours cannot be learned in an enclosure.

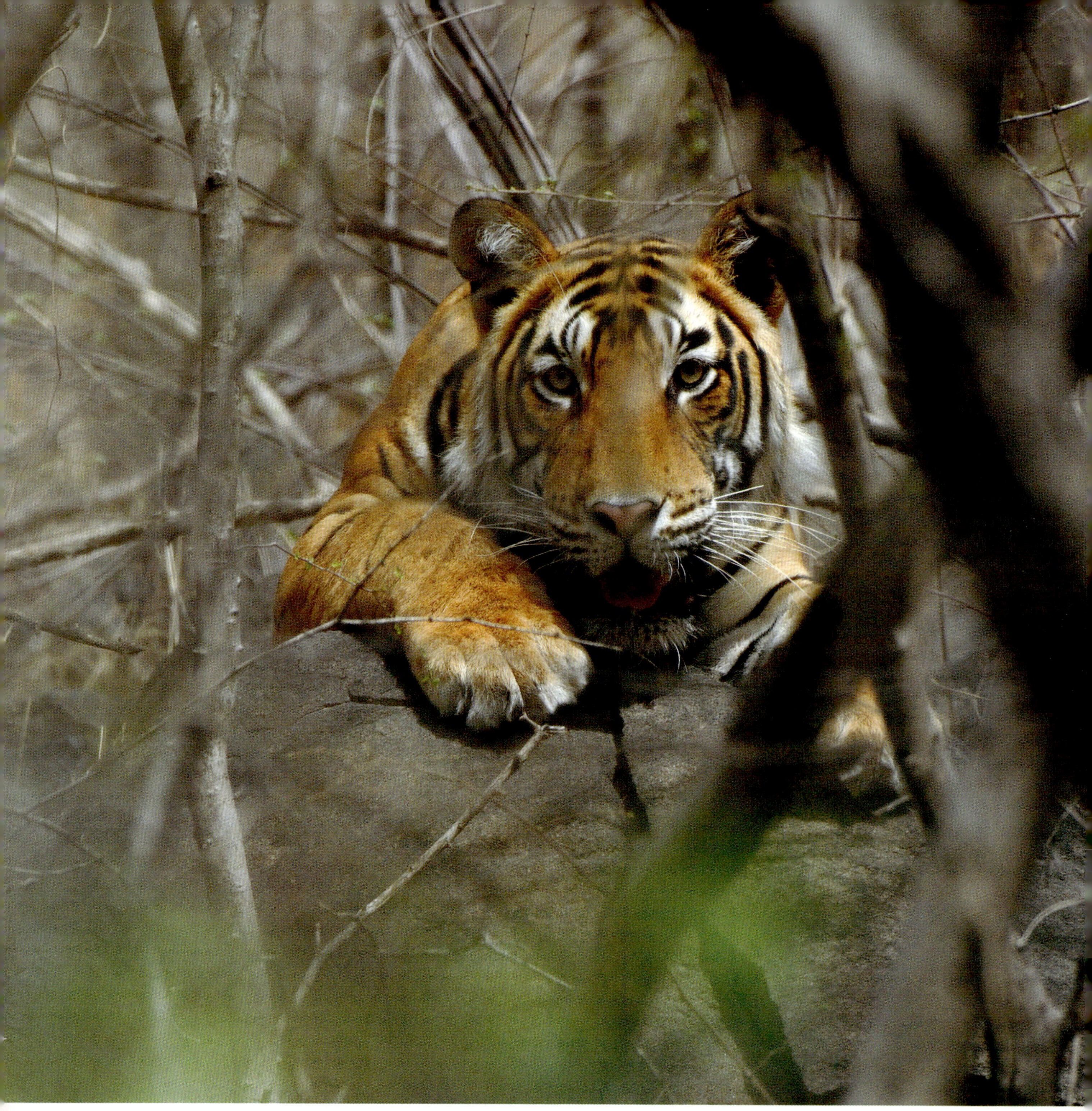

In 2008, a male captured in Ranthambhore National Park was transported there by helicopter. For the time being he has been put in an enclosure so that he can become accustomed to his new surroundings. If all goes well, he will be released and others will follow with a view to repopulating this area. The operation is a test case. If all the right conditions come together, tigers are resilient enough to recolonise lost lands which man has confiscated and is now in part giving back to them. For some decades, Siberian tigers have benefitted from a serious and structured support and protection programme in the Russian provinces of Khabarovsk and Primorsk, along the coast of the Sea of Japan.

It is becoming more and more difficult to link up the tiger populations in the individual Indian reserves. Each group needs to be large enough to sustain itself and provide a healthy amount of genetic variation.

"Regarding the old Project Tiger, I would say we need more science in the management of tigers: actions have to be based on scientific understanding of their needs, not just emotions. I think wild tiger populations will survive into the next century, if we act rationally. This means protecting tigers and their prey in 3 per cent of the land they occupy now, which does not mean giving up all development. I am hopeful that there will be places where people do sensible things and save tigers. But there should be more investment in promoting voluntary relocation of people away from critical tiger habitats, greater focus on protecting the tiger's prey base and greater use of science in monitoring the results of tiger conservation efforts. Man should be able to cohabit with big cats: as more and more of the world's population lives in urbanised areas, there will hopefully be a stronger basis of public support for tigers and less pressure on their habitats as people move away from land-based occupations."

K. Ullas Karanth, Ph. D. Senior Conservation Scientist-Wildlife Conservation Society & Director, Centre for Wildlife Studies, Bangalore, India

The programme extends into the extreme east of Manchuria, the mountains of Sikhote and Alin, part of the Amur and Ussuri river basins and Lake Khanka. Less good news is that no recent data is available on the tiger's status in North Korea. Among the arsenal of measures deployed to safeguard the supercat, it has been proposed to release some tigers into secure places, including some outside their countries of origin. In fact this has already been tried in some private reserves in southern Africa. In the Republic of South Africa there are vast national parks such as Kruger (20,000 km^2/7,800 sq. miles) which, like all the others in that country, are entirely enclosed. The wild animals live on one side of the fence, agriculture and human activity takes place on the other. There are also several private reserves of more modest dimensions, some of them adjoining the larger protected areas.

A yawning tiger is not necessarily bored. Yawning is a way of baring the teeth and showing off these formidable assets. It can also relieve tension when the animal has been watched for too long by humans kitted out with binoculars and cameras!

In these properties, you can either observe the animals or hunt them, for a fee in both cases. The animals are usually but not always local species and the environment is managed according to what each reserve wishes to attract. It is into this sort of reserve that tigers have been released and brought face to face with African antelope. They have demonstrated quite clearly that they can get by under these circumstances. But is this very different from a zoo? Is it an answer? Since the industrial revolution of the 19th century, modern economic development has always neglected ecology.

The most critical question is how to balance ecological and economic needs in the long term

A tiger stretches and yawns... How could anyone contemplating this magnificent creature fail to respect its way of life or not wish to understand an animal that asks nothing more than to live the way it has always lived?

The current economic climate shows that that is becoming less and less possible. Reserves of unsustainable resources such as fossil fuels seem to be running out. We are using up so-called sustainable resources such as forests and sea fish so quickly that they do not have enough breathing space to re-establish themselves. The impact of global climate change makes it essential that we start taking ecology into account. That could enable the tigers, the forests where they make their home and the neighbouring human populations to move from a no-win to a win-win situation. The exploitation of Malaysian forests may not be incompatible with the presence of tigers on the peninsula, nor of orangutans in Borneo. It will require studies integrating ecological impact and economic consequences, but this might find answers to the questions posed by the tiger and indeed by all the natural habitats on the planet. Transforming these venerable tropical forests into palm-oil plantations destroys a true source of wealth without solving the economic problems of the local people. In a world in disarray the oil palm alone cannot provide the evolutionary and adaptive potential represented by the thousands of species of plants and animals in the ancient tropical forests, by no means all of which have yet been identified. Knowing that tigers are still criss-crossing the undergrowth is a real ray of hope for the future, and not just the everyday life, of the forest and the human populations. Taking development in this new direction cannot be done in isolation; it must be undertaken at a global level. The tiger's image belongs to men of good will.

'But let me tell you this, my old friend: in a world made entirely for the benefit of man, it could well be that there is no longer room for man either.'
Romain Gary, *Letter to the Elephant,* 1968

Recommended reading

- Arsenyev V. (2000) *Dersu Uzala*. McPherson & Co., Kingston, New York.
- Baïkov N. (2002) *Des tigres et des hommes. 'Le Grand Van' et autres nouvelles*. Payot, Paris.
- Baïkov N. (2002) *Dans les collines de Mandchourie*. Payot, Paris.
- Bedi R., Bedi R. (1984) *Indian wildlife*. Collins Harvill,
- Can ÖE (2004) *Status, conservation and management of large carnivores in Turkey*. Convention on the conservation of European wildlife and natural habitats. Council of Europe, Strasbourg.
- Chapron G., Miquelle D.G., Lambert A., Goodrich J.M., Legendre S., Clobert J. (2008) 'The impact on tigers of poaching versus prey depletion'. *J. Appl. Ecol.* 45 : 1667-1674.
- Cubitt G., Mountfort G. (1985) *Wild India*. Collins, London.
- Driscoll C.A., Yamaguchi N., Bar-Gal G.K., Roca A.L., Luo S., Macdonald D.W., O'Brien S.J. (2009) 'Mitochondrial phylogeography illuminates the origin of the extinct Caspian tiger and its relationship to the Amur Tiger'. PloS ONE, 4(1), e4125 on line.
- Hawkins R.E. (1978) *Jim Corbett's India*. Oxford University Press, Oxford.
- Heptner V.G., Sludskii A.A. (1992) *Mammals of the Soviet Union: Carnivora Part 2, (Hyaenas and cats)*. E.J. Brill, Leiden.
- Inskip C., Zimmermann A. (2009) 'Human-felid conflict: a review of patterns and priorities worldwide'. *Oryx,* 43 (1) : 18-34.
- Israel S., Sinclair T. (eds.) (1988) *Indian wildlife*. Apa publications, Singapore.
- Matthiessen P. (2000) *Tigers in the Snow*. Harvill Press, London.
- Miller S.D., Everett D.D. (eds.) (1986) *Cats of the World: biology, conservation, management*. National Wildlife Federation, Washington DC.
- Sankhala K. (1977) *Tiger!* Simon & Schuster, New York.
- Schaller G.B. (1967) *The Deer and the Tiger*. University of Chicago Press, Chicago.
- Seidensticker J., Christie S., Jackson P. (eds.) (1999) *Riding the Tiger*. Cambridge University Press, Cambridge.
- Sunquist F., Sunquist M. (1988) *Tiger Moon: tracking the great cats of Nepal*. University of Chicago Press, Chicago.
- Sunquist M., Sunquist F. (2002) *Wild Cats of the World*. University of Chicago Press, Chicago.
- Thapar V. (1990) *Tigers: the secret life*. Elm Tree Books, London.
- Tilson R.L., Seal U.S. (eds.) (1987) *Tigers of the World*. Noyes Publications, Park Ridge, New Jersey.
- Turner A., Anton M. (1997) *The big cats and their fossil relatives*. Columbia University Press, New York.
- Wilson D.E., Mittermeier R. (eds.) (2009) *Handbook of the mammals of the world. Volume I. Carnivores*. Lynx edicions, Barcelona.

Further information

- Tigris Foundation: http://www.tigrisfoundation.nl/cms/publish/content/showpage.asp?themeid=1
- Carnivore Conservation: http://www.carnivoreconservation.org/portal/index.php
- IUCN/Species Survival Commission Cat Specialist Group: http://www.catsg.org/catsgportal/20_catsg-website/home/index_en.htm
- People and Wildlife: creating conservation solutions for living together: http://www.peopleandwildlife.org.uk/
- The tiger page on the IUCN Red List of Threatened Species: http://www.iucnredlist.org/details/15955/0

Acknowledgements

This book would never have seen the light of day without the encouragement and patience of Christine Baillet.

François Moutou is very grateful to Belinda Wright, Executive Director of the Wildlife Protection Society of India, Dr Ullas Karanth, Wildlife Conservation Society, Bangalore, India, and Bittu Saghal, Sanctuary Magazine, Mumbai, India, who agreed to answer his questions and fill in gaps in his research. He would also like to thank the photographer Alain Pons, who trusted him to write the words that accompany his magnificent images. François Moutou also thanks Caroline Taggart for translating his Gallic text into fine English.

To produce such images, you need to do more than go to a country, pay an entrance fee to a national park and photograph what passes in front of the lens. It is a long-term project requiring many visits and even more hours looking for and waiting for the animals. So it needs both patience and passion, but that isn't all. In this respect, Alain Pons wishes to thank all the people who, through their help and friendship, made it easier for him to observe the big cat, particularly Véronique and Raghu in Delhi, Pappu and Raj in Bandhavgarh and Vipul and Satish in Ranthambhore. Many thanks, too, to Pierre Gay of the Doué-la-Fontaine biopark and to Patrick Jardin of Parc des Félins at Nesles who enabled him to complete this book.

Alain Pons' photos were all taken in the Indian national parks of Ranthambore, Bandhavgarh, Kahna, Corbett and Kaziranga, except:
Sumatran tiger pages 14 (top left), 30 and 116 (top): Doué-la-Fontaine biopark, France; page 108 (top right): Parc des Félins, Nesles, France
Bengal tiger page 82 (bottom left): Parc des Félins, Nesles, France; page 116 (bottom): Parc de Saint-Vrain, France
White tiger pages 108 and 118: Parc des Félins, Nesles, France
Siberian tiger pages 14 (bottom) and 26: Lazovsky Preserve at Lazo and Uthos Rehabilitation Centre, near Khabarovsk, Russia
Tiger farm page 108: Xiogsen Bear and Tiger Park, Guilin, China

OTHER *Wild things...* TITLES

Wild Things...
Creatures of the Deep Blue
ISBN: 978-1-901268-34-8

Wild Things...
The Great Apes
ISBN: 978-1-901268-31-7

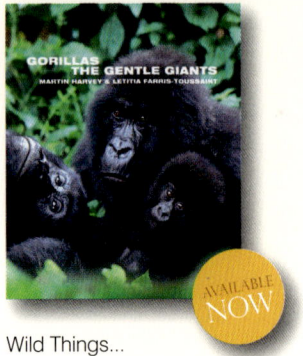

Wild Things...
Gorillas – The Gentle Giants
ISBN: 978-1-901268-35-5

Other wildlife titles published by Evans Mitchell Books

www.embooks.co.uk

Wildlife Monographs
Snow Monkeys
ISBN: 978-1-901268-34-8

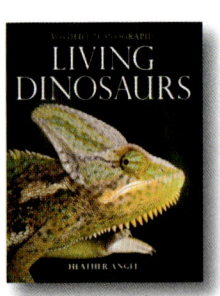

Wildlife Monographs
Living Dinosaurs
ISBN: 978-1-901268-36-2

Wildlife Monographs
Giant Pandas
ISBN: 978-1-901268-13-3

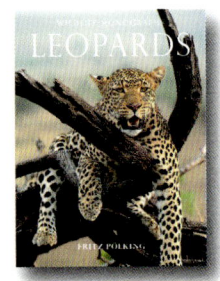

Wildlife Monographs
Loepards
ISBN: 978-1-901268-12-6

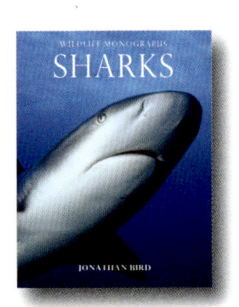

Wildlife Monographs
Sharks
ISBN: 978-1-901268-11-9

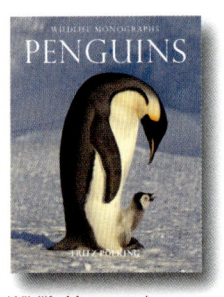

Wildlife Monographs
Penguins
ISBN: 978-1-901268-14-0

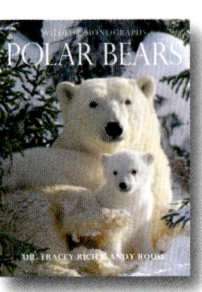

Wildlife Monographs
Polar Bears
ISBN: 978-1-901268-15-7

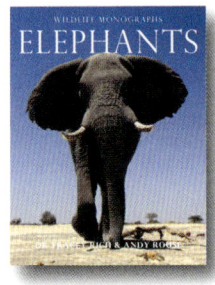

Wildlife Monographs
Elephants
ISBN: 978-1-901268-08-9

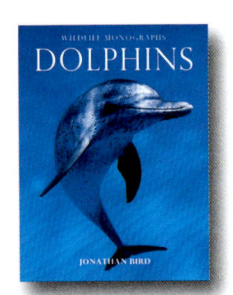

Wildlife Monographs
Dolphins
ISBN: 978-1-901268-17-1

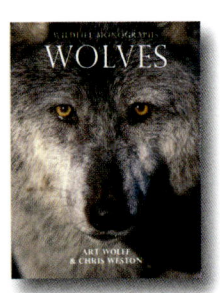

Wildlife Monographs
Wolves
ISBN: 978-1-901268-18-8

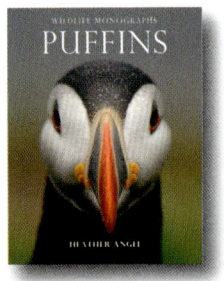

Wildlife Monographs
Puffins
ISBN: 978-1-901268-19-5

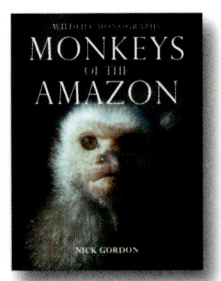

Wildlife Monographs
Monkeys of the Amazon
ISBN: 978-1-901268-10-2

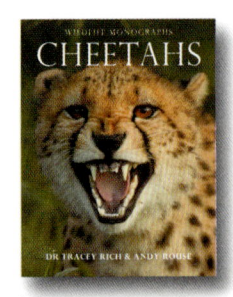

Wildlife Monographs
Cheetahs
ISBN: 978-1-901268-09-6